SaY

The Weird and Mysterious Journey of the English Language

WhAt?

GENA K. GORRELL

TUNDRA BOOKS

Published in Canada by Tundra Books,
75 Sherbourne Street, Toronto, Ontario M5A 2P9

Published in the United States by Tundra Books of Northern New York,
P.O. Box 1030, Plattsburgh, New York 12901

Library of Congress Control Number: 2009928409

Library and Archives Canada Cataloguing in Publication

Gorrell, Gena K. (Gena Kinton), 1946-
    Say what? : the weird and mysterious journey of the English language / Gena K. Gorrell.

Includes index.
ISBN 978-0-88776-878-1

    1. English language--History--Juvenile literature. I. Title.

PE1075.G675 2009   j420.9   C2009-902917-0

We acknowledge the financial support of the Government of Canada through the Book Publishing Industry Development Program (BPIDP) and that of the Government of Ontario through the Ontario Media Development Corporation's Ontario Book Initiative. We further acknowledge the support of the Canada Council for the Arts and the Ontario Arts Council for our publishing program.

ONTARIO ARTS COUNCIL
CONSEIL DES ARTS DE L'ONTARIO

Printed and bound in Canada

This book is printed on acid-free paper that is 100% recycled, ancient-forest friendly (40% post-consumer recycled).

1 2 3 4 5 6   14 13 12 11 10 09

This book is dedicated to my father,
Jack Muir, who was always my best editor,
and who taught me from the beginning
that "Well, you know what I mean" is

just

not

good

enough.

Language is the memory of the human race.

                                                 — WILLIAM HENRY SMITH

Contents

Introduction

THE PUZZLE OF ENGLISH

Where on earth did the English language come from? Over a million words, and such weird spellings! Aren't there any rules? Some words are spelled the same but said differently ("The **wind** made the flag **wind** around the pole"). Others are spelled differently but pronounced the same ("Did you bring **enough stuff**?") How did English get so complicated?

The answer is that English isn't just the speech of one nation; it's the memory of thousands of years of history. It tracks the places people came from and the places they went to; the adventures they had; the friends and enemies they made; the battles they won and lost. It marks the days when legions of Roman soldiers stomped onto England's shore – the days when Viking warriors sailed their dragon boats across the sea to plunder British villages – the day a king of England was felled by an arrow on the battlefield and a foreigner seized his throne. As English changed and grew, it became a jumble of sounds and words and rules from countless languages and lands. And it's still changing, still growing, every day.

> **How many ways do we spell the sound "sh"?**
> There's <u>sh</u>op and <u>s</u>ure; man<u>si</u>on and po<u>ti</u>on; ti<u>ss</u>ue, o<u>ce</u>an, <u>ch</u>ampagne, fu<u>ch</u>sia (a flower), an<u>ci</u>ent, con<u>sci</u>ous, and <u>sch</u>ist (a kind of rock). And think of the "o" sound in **so**, **sew**, and **sow**. Can you find seven other ways to spell that sound?
> (The answers are at the end of this chapter.)

If you want an example, look at Tolkien's novel *The Hobbit*. When Bilbo Baggins first meets the wizard Gandalf, the hobbit exclaims:

> Gandalf, Gandalf! Good gracious me! . . . Not the fellow who used to tell such wonderful tales at parties, about dragons and goblins and giants and the rescue of princesses . . . ?

That looks like plain English, doesn't it? But **gracious** and **princess** both come from Latin – *gratia*, "kindness," and *princeps*, "leader." **Dragon** and **giant** are from Greek *drakon* and *gigant*. **Fellow** and **wonderful** come from the Norse spoken by those ancient Viking warriors. As for **Gandalf**, it's Norse for "wand-elf"!

English has words from languages so old that we

barely know they existed. It has words from prehistoric tribes, and from today's languages – from Hindi, Arabic, and Chinese; from the Choctaws in North America, the Guaranís in South America, and the Aboriginals in Australia. More than seventy percent of all English words were born someplace other than England. Spin a globe and put your finger down on almost any patch of land; English has words that come from there.

That's why the language can be so confusing and inconsistent. That's why, for every rule about English, there's a fistful of exceptions. And that's why this is the richest, most international, most versatile language in the world.

1

THE MOTHER TONGUE

Where did language start in the first place? It must have been long before there were humans. Imagine primitive ape-creatures huddled together in a cave; they'd have to communicate somehow. They'd want some way to say, *Give that back, it's mine!* or *Move over, you're standing on my foot!* And the more they lived together, the more they'd need to say. *Where'd you find those blueberries? Chase that rabbit over here and I'll grab it.* As they evolved into humans, and learned farming and other skills, their language would become more complicated: *I'll trade you half my honey next week for one of those catfish today.*

While early humans were developing languages, they were also migrating from place to place. Sometimes they were driven by changes in the weather, or by natural disasters like floods and forest fires. Sometimes they were moving away from hostile neighbors, or following the animals they hunted. For many reasons, groups of people were leaving one home territory and looking for another.

By comparing certain languages and tracing their roots, finding similar words that seem to come from the same ancient, mysterious source, scholars have concluded that in the far distant past – maybe six or eight thousand years ago – some people were speaking a language that has now been lost. They had no writing (that we've found) so we have no records, and we know very little about who they were, or where and how they lived. They seem to have had words for **snow** and **wolf** but not for **ocean**, so their homeland was probably cold and far from the sea – likely somewhere in Central Europe. But that's about all we can say. That, and one other thing: for some reason, small bands of these people migrated in different directions. They carried their language across Europe and Asia and even up into Scandinavia.

Once their communities became separated, their ways of speaking slowly began to differ, creating a whole family of languages that we describe as Indo-European. One version, Celtic Indo-European, is the source of modern Welsh, and of the Gaelic spoken in Ireland and Scotland. Farther south, Greek Indo-European developed into ancient and then modern Greek. The Indo-Iranian form is the foundation of most languages of India, Pakistan, and Iran. Italic Indo-European gave rise to Latin, which gave rise to Italian, French, and Spanish. The Slavic version is the basis of Russian, Bulgarian, and Polish. Germanic Indo-European is the root of Dutch, most Scandinavian languages, German and

How much Sanskrit is hiding in your kitchen? The ancient Hindus cooked with *pippali* (berry), *sarkara* (grit), and *crngaveram* (powdered horn-body, an antler-shaped root). The Greeks called these seasonings *peperi*, *sakkharon*, and *ziggiberis*. We know them as **pepper**, **sugar**, and **ginger**. (Do you see where the artificial sweetener **saccharin** gets its name?)

Yiddish – and English. And these are only a few examples. Altogether, the roots of the languages spoken by about half the people in today's world reach back to the Indo-European tongue of those unknown people so long ago.

One of the earliest Indo-European languages that we have in written form is Sanskrit. In India, Hindu scriptures called the Veda were written in Sanskrit about 3,500 years ago. (*Veda* is Sanskrit for "knowledge.") Sanskrit was the language of India's court and literature 2,500 years ago, and although it's not used in daily speech any more, it's still part of Hindu religious ceremonies.

Although modern Indo-European languages have been developing separately for thousands of years, and now seem very different from one another, it's intriguing to track down the similarities. For example, the Sanskrit words for **one**, **two**, **three**, are pronounced *eka, dvi, tri*. Compare those ancient words to these:

	1	2	3
Greek	*en*	*duo*	*treis*
Latin	*unus*	*duus*	*tres*
French	*un*	*deux*	*trois*
Italian	*uno*	*due*	*tre*
Spanish	*uno*	*dos*	*tres*
German	*ein*	*zwei*	*drei*
Portuguese	*um*	*dois*	*tres*
Dutch	*een*	*twee*	*drie*
Danish	*en*	*to*	*tre*

And look at the "family tree" for this word:

Sanskrit *bhratr*

Greek *phrater* Irish *brathair*

French *frère* Latin *frater*

Welsh *brawd* Italian *fratello*

German *Bruder* Dutch *broeder*

English *brother*

One of the greatest Hindu gods, Shiva (*SHEE-vah*), appears in Sanskrit texts over two thousand years old. Shiva can take various forms, some kind, some cruel and dreadful. Here he appears as the four-armed Lord of the Dance, surrounded by a fiery halo representing the cycle of creation, destruction, and rebirth, and trampling a demon to symbolize the end of evil.

Sanskrit and its descendants – such as Latin, Ancient Greek, and early French and Germanic languages – gave English more than just vocabulary. They also left fragments of their grammar, ghosts that lurk behind our sentences like scraps of faded photos in a family album. These odds and ends can be puzzling, even frustrating, but they deserve respect. They come from the dawn of the English language, and long before.

2 THE GLORY THAT WAS GREECE

Greece is a smallish country, about the size of England – and like England, it was once the heart of an empire. At its height, starting around 500 BCE (Before the Christian Era), Greece boasted magnificent architecture, painting, and sculpture. Its poets and playwrights were renowned across Europe. Education was greatly prized, and orators (public speakers) who were logical and eloquent were celebrated as heroes.

As the Greeks sailed their ships along the shores of the Mediterranean Sea, setting up colonies to trade their wine, olive oil, and pottery for products such as wheat and metals, their language became known as far away as Spain and North Africa.

In the mid-300s BCE, the brilliant military campaigns of the young king Alexander the Great spread Greek civilization and culture to even more distant lands – down the Nile River through Egypt, and east into India.

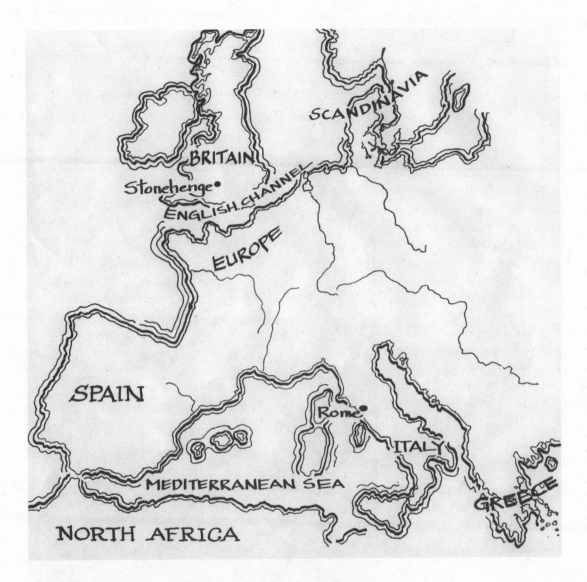

The Greek language was used in government as well as in fashionable, artistic circles. It was also handy as a lingua franca – a common language understood by traders and travelers from many different places.

One reason for the success of the language was the Greek alphabet. Earlier cultures had found ways to write words, but their systems were generally very complicated and required a lot of fancy symbols, usually based on pictures. All those symbols were hard to learn, and they weren't easy to copy out, either.

This pillar marks the tomb of a high-ranking priest-scribe at an Egyptian pharaoh's court more than four thousand years ago. The Ancient Egyptians had about seven hundred hieroglyphic signs, each representing a consonant or a mix of consonants. (They didn't write vowel sounds.) The symbols inside the cartouche (oval line, upper left and middle right) represent a flowering reed, a feather, a hare, and water, and spell out the pharaoh's name. Hieroglyphs were elegant and decorative, but only a few people — mostly priest-scribes — could read them.

But another ancient civilization – the Phoenicians, who lived about where Lebanon is now – had had the brilliant idea of using a handful of simple signs to represent consonants. (The Phoenicians and the Egyptians didn't bother writing vowels.) The Greeks had adapted this system sometime around the 800s BCE, adding a few vowels and other sounds and ending up with about twenty-four letters. And there it was: a quick, efficient way to write a letter or a shopping list or a poem, and so easy that a schoolchild could learn it. And this set of letters began: *a*, *b* – alpha, beta.

What word can you make out of A-B-C-D? **Abecedarian**, meaning something related to the alphabet, or someone learning it. "Isn't little Sally clever? She's only three, and already she's an abecedarian."

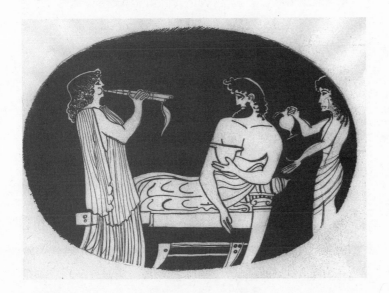

The Greeks were seen as highly cultured, and experts in life's little pleasures — good food, fine wine, music, and romance. They decorated pottery bowls and vases with scenes from daily life, historical events, and the endless shenanigans of their gods.

After Alexander died suddenly when he was only thirty-three, his empire began to collapse. In time, the remnants of Greece were swallowed up by the Roman Empire. But the Romans themselves had been nourished by the culture of Greece. The Roman alphabet was derived from the Greek alphabet. The Roman language,

"The art of speaking enchants the soul," declared Plato (427?-347? BCE), a writer and philosopher, and one of the most famous Greeks. He also pointed out that "An orator's virtue is to speak the truth."

Latin, had been influenced by Greek. Roman literature was patterned after the works of Greece. Educated Romans were expected to be fluent in Greek; for less privileged people, Greek plays, poems, and speeches were translated into Latin. Children of wealthy Roman families studied under Greek tutors, and often completed their education by traveling in Greece.

The Greek gods lived on Mount Olympus and led soap-opera lives of passion, deceit, jealousy, and revenge. Nemesis was a goddess who punished those who were evil, arrogant, or vain. Today, a **nemesis** is a supreme enemy or destroyer. (Harry Potter is Lord Voldemort's nemesis.)

In Greek mythology, when Halcyone found her drowned husband's body on the shore, she was so heartbroken that she drowned herself. Halcyone and her husband were turned into kingfishers, birds that were thought to nest on a calm sea. That's why calm and peaceful times are called **halcyon** (*HAL-see-on*) days.

In the centuries that followed, the writings of the ancient Greeks – myths, fables, plays, and philosophy – shaped European society. Well into the 1800s, people could hardly claim to be educated unless they read at least a little Greek.

3 ECHOES OF ANCIENT GREEK

The Greek alphabet often shows up in our maths and sciences: **beta** blockers are a class of medications, **gamma** rays are a kind of electromagnetic radiation, and **pi** (π, the Greek letter *p*) is a ratio used in math involving circles. The leaders of an animal pack are the **alpha** female and **alpha** male. A triangular airplane wing, or the triangle of a spreading river-mouth, is a **delta**, after the capital Greek *D*, Δ. (You can find the whole Greek alphabet in "More about Greek," at the end of this book.)

We borrow Greek words to create all kinds of new meanings. The Greek for **circle**, *kuklos*, shows up in **bicycle**, **cyclone** (a circular storm), and **recycling** (using over and over). From *naus*, **ship**, we get **nautical** (related to ships and sailing), navigable (passable by ships – "Is that river navigable?"), and astronaut ("star-sailor"). From *hudor* (water) come **dehydrated** (deprived of water), **hydraulic** (powered by water), and **hydroponics** (growing plants in

Iota was the name of the Greek *i*, the smallest letter in their alphabet. In English an **iota** is the smallest possible amount ("She hasn't got an iota of talent!") Our word **jot** comes from *iota*, and means the same thing. And when we "jot down a note," we are writing as little as possible.

water without soil). Knowing a little Greek can help you figure out a lot of English words, even if you've never seen them before.

> The Greeks had two versions of the letter o. One was *omicron* (o), or o-little (as in "microscope," for seeing little things). The other was *omega* (Ω), or o-big (as in "megacity," big city). Since omega was the last letter of the Greek alphabet, "My dog knows every trick from alpha to omega" means Rover knows all the tricks from A to Z – in other words, absolutely everything.
>
> In Ancient Greece, male athletes practiced their exercises naked (*gumnos*). We still call a room for athletics a **gymnasium**.

The Greek alphabet may have been simple, but the language certainly wasn't. It was highly "inflected" – that is, words changed depending on how they were used. A noun could have many forms, because if you wrote "This crocodile stole the fish from that crocodile and gave it to another crocodile," the ending on "crocodile" was different each time, depending on what role that particular crocodile played in the action. If you said "These crocodiles" you needed a whole different set of endings, for the plural. And if you talked about one lion (*leon*) or two lions instead of one or two crocodiles, you needed two more sets of endings, because words ending in *os* (like *krokodilos*) didn't have the same endings as words ending

in *on* (like *leon*) – in the singular, or in the plural!

And that's only the beginning. All nouns also had gender. **Grasshopper** was masculine but **flea** was feminine. **Soup** was masculine but **dessert** was neuter (neither masculine nor feminine). So if you described some animal as large (*megas*), the ending on *megas* depended on how many animals you meant, and whether they were masculine or feminine or neuter, and what role they played in the action!

And verbs were no easier. We say **come** and **coming** and **came**, and we add a few auxiliary verbs (such as **was**, **will**, or **had**). A Greek verb could have as many as *two hundred* different forms, depending on the tense (past, present, future, etc.), the voice (active or passive), how many people were involved, and so on.

How did schoolkids ever learn all those endings? *Memorize, memorize, memorize!*

In Ancient Greek, *kroke* means "stones" and *drilos* means "worm" — so a worm-shaped animal that liked to sunbathe on stony shores was called a *krokodilos*.

Here are a few Greek words and their meanings. Can you match the English terms below to their definitions?

γη *ge* earth

'ηλιος *helios* sun

κρυος *kruos* cold

κρυπτος *kruptos* hidden

πυρ *pur* fire

ταχυς *tachus* fast

θεος *theos* god

1) cryogenics

2) tachometer

3) geothermal

4) heliocentrism

5) theocracy

6) pyromaniac

7) cryptogram

8) tachycardia

9) cryptozoology

10) heliotrope

11) cryobiology

12) pantheism

a) an abnormally fast heartbeat

b) belief in many gods, or in God within everything

c) an instrument that measures how fast an engine is working

d) a kind of flower that turns to keep facing the sun

e) the study of the effects of extreme cold on living things

f) the search for and study of animals that may not exist (such as Bigfoot)

g) the study of the production and effects of extreme cold

h) someone obsessed with setting fires

i) related to the earth's internal temperature

j) government by a god (or priesthood)

k) considering the sun to be the center of everything

l) a message disguised by a code or some other system

ANSWERS

WORDS FROM GREEK

1-**g**

2-**c** metron is Greek for "measure" — as in "metric"

3-**i** as in "thermometer"

4-**k**

5-**j** as in "democracy," run by the demos, people

6-**h**

7-**l** as in "telegram," a message from far away, tele

8-**e**

9-**f**

10-**d** trepein is Greek for "turn"

11-**e**

12-**b** pan means "all" — a "panacea" is a medicine that supposedly cures all diseases

Euphemisms (from Greek *eu pheme,* "fine-speaking") are polite ways of not saying what we really mean — and we work them overtime when it comes to certain bodily functions. Our word "toilet" is from French *toilette,* dressing room. The Romans went to the *necessarium*; we go to the washroom, but not just to wash; to the bathroom, but not to bathe; to the powder room, but not to powder anything! We go to the ladies' and gents', the little room, the bog (wet like a swamp), the privy (private place), the john. In England we pop out to the WC (water closet), lavatory (from French *laver,* to wash,) or loo (perhaps from French *l'eau,* "water," or *lieu,* "place"). And if we need to "spend a penny," we're recalling the days when many public toilets in England were behind a one-penny turnstile.

4

BRITANNIA, PROVINCIA ROMANA

Sometime around thirty-five hundred years ago, people in Britain built Stonehenge and other monuments out of giant, roughly carved stones. We're still not sure what these constructions were used for, and we don't know what language people spoke as they worked together on these huge projects.

We don't know when humans first arrived in England, or how they lived. We do know that by about 2,500 years ago, they were not only using stone and copper tools; they also were mixing copper and tin to make bronze, for tools and weapons that were stronger and lasted longer. But over in Europe, some tribes called Celts were even more advanced. They had learned to make tools and weapons out of iron, which was stronger than bronze. They had mastered the art of riding horses, and harnessing them to chariots.

By 700 BCE, small bands of Celts were sailing from Europe to England as traders or settlers. Larger and larger groups followed. The native Britons, the Stonehenge-builders, tried to resist the invaders, but they were defeated again and again.

More Celts flooded in, building great earthen castles on hilltops, and fortifying them with high walls and deep ditches. They were ruled by priests and by fierce warriors who fought on horseback or from chariots, cloaked in bronze armor and brandishing iron weapons. Celtic artisans crafted ornate jewelry, wove fine fabrics that they colored with vegetable dyes, and made fragrant soaps and lotions and perfumes. Fleets of Celtic merchant ships carried goods to distant kingdoms, to be traded for exotic novelties.

The Celts' language, religion, and folklore spread across much of Britain with them. Celtic was not a written language, but Celtic bards (storytellers) knew endless ballads of adventure and romance to enthrall their listeners. For hundreds of years Britain was dominated by the Celts, yet only a few English words come from Celtic – including **Britain**, from *Prydein*.

But while the Britons and Celts were learning to live together, sometimes fighting, sometimes intermarrying, a new empire was creeping toward their shores. The city-state of Rome had overgrown its boundaries and spilled out into the rest of Italy. Rome's armies were on the march, fighting their way across one land after another, building an empire. The well-armed Roman legions became renowned for their discipline and organization. Building a great navy, Rome spread its rule into France, Spain, and Africa. In 146 BCE, Rome conquered Greece. A hundred years later, Roman territories circled the entire coast of the Mediterranean. And wherever the Romans went, they took Latin as the language of law and government, and Greek as the language of the arts.

In 55 and 54 BCE, Julius Caesar led the first two Roman invasions into Britain. Some ninety years later – in

Celtic weapons and armor were often decorated with superbly crafted metal and enamel, and precious stones like coral and amber. This bronze shield, with its pattern of elegant curlicues, is studded with disks of red glass.

43 AD – forty thousand Roman troops braved the sea crossing for a massive attack. By 67 AD, four legions (about twenty thousand soldiers) were posted in Rome's new province of Britannia.

Caius Julius Caesar (100?-44 BCE) was not only a Roman general but a brilliant statesman, writer, and orator. He was also a military genius, and he expanded the empire so spectacularly that later Roman emperors also called themselves Caesar. Various forms of the name now mean "emperor" in other countries: **Kaiser** in Germany, and **czar** (or **tsar**) in Russia.

Castra is Latin for **army camp**. Today, the names of many English towns – Lancaster, Cirencester, Winchester – mark them as places where Roman soldiers lived almost two thousand years ago.

In time, Rome took over much of Britain, well up into what is now Scotland. Roman troops were kept busy suppressing rebellions from within the province, repelling cross-border raids by Celtic tribes on the north and west, and fending off raids by seafaring Germanic tribes along the south and east.

But the Romans were a practical, businesslike people. Once they more or less controlled Britannia, they focused

Roman soldiers were tough, highly trained professionals who used expert tactics against their many enemies. By locking their shields into this tank-like *testudo* ("tortoise") formation, for example, they could stay protected while attacking an enemy position.

on matters of trade and government (especially tax-collecting!) The result was the Pax Romana, or Roman Peace (27 BCE to 180 AD), a fairly calm and prosperous interval after so many years of warfare.

The Romans built fortified towns as refuges for times of rebellion, warehouses to protect trade goods, safe harbors for their ships. They laid out long, straight, solidly built roads, with stone bridges and distance-markers, so their armies and supplies could travel swiftly. Then they turned their attention to the details of everyday life: aqueducts to bring water to towns and garrisons, and sewers to take it away; temples and statues to please the many Roman gods; theaters and amphitheaters for entertainment; public toilets and bathhouses; lavish villas for the wealthy. Towns grew into cities, and little villages blossomed into towns.

The Romans did their best to spread Latin and the Roman culture in the province. Roman-style schools were set up, to teach elite British boys. It was difficult to succeed in business, at least in the towns and cities, without

"Great Caesar's ghost!" exclaimed Superman's boss at the *Daily Planet* newspaper, when he was excited. Most of us use exclamations that don't mean anything except that we're astonished or angry or we've stepped on a wasp. Each culture has its own exclamations, many of them not too polite. When religion dominates daily life, expressions like **damn** or **hell** are forbidden (people get around that with inventions like **dang** or **darn** or **heck**). At other times, quite innocent body parts (legs, for example) have been seen as offensive. Today, various body parts and functions are considered unmentionable – so we won't mention them!

speaking passable Latin. Britons enlisted in the Roman legions, to serve at home and abroad; aging Roman soldiers acquired land in Britannia, and built themselves retirement estates. One way and another, Latin became part of the Britons' life, especially around Londinium (London). But in the countryside, and farther north and west, Celtic remained the language of the land.

> The Romans had countless gods and goddesses, and they are with us still. **Cereals** are named for Ceres, goddess of grain harvests. **Flora** and **fauna**, the plants and animals of a particular area, are named for Flora, goddess of flowers, and Fauna, sister of Faunus, a god of woods and forests. And **vulcanizing** – treating something (like a rubber tire) at high temperatures to make it hard and durable – is named for Vulcan, god of fire. His name also gives us **volcanoes**, and **volcanology** or **vulcanology**, the science of volcanoes.

Meanwhile, things were happening back in Rome. All those colorful, quarrelsome gods were being challenged by the single god of a new religion, Christianity. Rome itself was being attacked by primitive tribes from the east. Weakened by corruption, bad government, and a host of other problems, the Roman Empire split into two sections, and its power declined. The troops occupying Britannia were withdrawn and sent to fight elsewhere. In 410 AD, Rome officially gave up its occupation of Britannia. By the late 400s, the days of the Ancient Roman Empire were over.

AMICUS, AMICE, AMICUM

On the other side of the English Channel, in the Roman provinces of Gaul and Iberia (France and Spain), Latin had gradually replaced most Celtic languages. (Italian, French, and Spanish are known as Romance languages because they developed from the language of the Romans.) But although Latin was Britain's language of law and government for some four hundred years, it never caught on among the common people. They continued to speak Celtic, with a sprinkling of handy Latin words.

What was Latin like? The Romans had adopted the Greek alphabet, dropping some letters, changing others, and rearranging the sequence. They ended up with pretty much the alphabet we use today.

Like Greek, Latin was highly inflected. Nouns, and the adjectives that described them, changed their endings depending on their number and gender and case (the role

Salt – mined from the ground or recovered from sea-water – used to be a precious commodity; that's why we call good people the **salt of the earth**. Salt seasoned many dishes people ate, and kept food from spoiling during the long, hungry months of winter. Domestic animals like cows and goats couldn't survive without it. The soldiers of the Roman armies were sometimes paid in salt (*sal* in Latin), giving us our word **salary**, and we still say that people who earn their pay are **worth their salt**. Greens with salt and other seasonings make a **salad**, and preserved meats are **salami**. All of this from salt!

played by the word). We often use a preposition to indicate the role: "*to* a friend, *from* a friend, *about* a friend"; the Romans could just change the ending, like this:

nominative (*subject of verb*) My <u>friend</u> (a*micus*) came.

vocative (*one spoken to*) "Hey, <u>friend</u> (a*mice*)!"

accusative (*direct object*) I gave <u>my friend</u> to the frog (*amicum*).

genitive (*possessive*) The father <u>of my friend</u> (*amici*) came.

dative (*indirect object*) I gave the frog <u>to my friend</u> (*amico*).

ablative (*other indirect connection*)
    My frog is <u>from my friend</u> (*amico*).

As in Greek, if the friend was a girl, or there were several boys, or several girls, or the word's nominative (subject) case didn't end in *us* (like *amicus*), the endings were different.

Compare this to English. Do we change endings for number, gender, and case? We usually change plurals, one way or another (**frog**, **frogs**; **mouse**, **mice**). We occasionally change endings to show gender (**actor**, **actress**; **waiter**, **waitress**), although this is going out of fashion. And we don't change adjectives at all – whether we're talking about one *rude* girl or ten *rude* boys!

When you study Latin, you learn how to "decline" the nouns – how to change them according to their use. Here's how you decline the word for "pig."

	singular	plural
nominative	porcus	porci
vocative	porce	porci
accusative	porcum	porcos
genitive	porci	porcorum
dative	porco	porcis
ablative	porco	porcis

Now, here's how we decline the word in English: pig pig pig pig's pig pig; pigs pigs pigs pigs' pigs pigs.

It's no wonder you don't find a lot of people speaking Latin these days!

We don't use all those case endings for nouns, but we do say, "My *friend's* glove," or the plural, "My *friends' house*." The apostrophe tells us that "friend" is in the possessive case. In fact, we can use three systems to show the role of a noun: that *s*, if it's possessive; a preposition (like **to** or **from**); or simply the order of the words. We can say, "I showed Jason's bike *to* Ali," or "I showed Ali Jason's bike," putting Ali first. (Because "I showed the cat the bird" is not the same as "I showed the bird the cat"!)

People sometimes confuse the possessive **s** with the plural **s**. This mistake so often appears on shop signs that it's known as the greengrocer's apostrophe. Another common mistake is to put an apostrophe in the possessive *its*. Remember: the possessive **his**, **hers**, and **its** have *no* apostrophe. **It's** is short for **it is**.

We still see Latin as a language of scholarship. Those spells that Harry Potter struggles to learn at Hogwarts are Latin, or at least mock-Latin – *Ferula! Lumos! Expelliarmus!*

When Harry forgets his Latin cases and cries, *"Expecto patrono"* instead of *"Expecto patronum,"* his patronus doesn't appear. (In Latin, a *patronus* is someone who protects people – like Harry's patronus, a dazzling silver stag that appears out of nowhere to drive away his enemies.)

Even today, some Latin words appear, unchanged, in English. *Campus* means "flat field." *Victor* means "winner." *Veto* ("I forbid") now means a rejection: "Your parents will **veto** your plan to go sky-diving." *Recipe* meant **take**; now, as well as telling you what ingredients to use and how to cook them, a **recipe** is a prescription for medicine (the "Rx" you see in drugstores is a short form for **recipe**). *Alibi* ("in another place"), *exit* ("he, she, or it leaves"), *ignoramus* ("we don't know") – see how much Latin you already know?

Latin is especially common in law courts. See if you can figure out these legal terms. First, here's some Latin vocabulary. Notice that the adjectives have three forms – masculine, feminine, and neuter.

bonus, bona, bonum	good
primus, prima, primum	first
pro	for
sub	under

Now try matching up these legal terms and their meanings;

1) **bona fide**

2) **subpoena**

3) **pro bono publico**
(often shortened to pro bono)

4) **pro forma**

5) **prima facie**

6) **sub judice**

a) under consideration in a court of law

b) to act in good faith
(not trying to cheat anyone)

c) for the good of the public
(for free, not for pay)

d) at first sight
(apparently, but not necessarily)

e) as a matter of form
(paperwork)

f) an order to attend court under
penalty if you don't come

ANSWERS

ANGLES AND SAXONS AND VIKINGS

After the Romans abandoned Britannia, life there changed for the worse. Without the Roman merchant fleet, international trade collapsed, and workshops ground to a halt. Without constant maintenance by the Roman army, roads and aqueducts fell into disrepair. With fewer jobs available, and not much law enforcement, there was more crime. Towns dwindled as people moved back to the countryside, to make a living any way they could.

The most serious threat, though, was from overseas. The Romans had fought vigilantly against pirates, raiders, and invaders from all sides. They had manned a chain of forts and watchtowers along the borders, and kept a fleet of warships nearby. Now, Britain's coast lay undefended.

By 440 CE, immigrants from Germanic tribes were beginning to arrive in Britain from northern Europe. Although they were expert seafarers and skilled farmers, they

Fewer jobs? Less jobs? Which is right? **Fewe**r refers to things counted in whole numbers; **less** is for things you might have just part of. You wash *fewer* than three teacups but you drink *less* than three cups of tea (maybe just two and a half). You go trick-or-treating at **fewer** than twenty houses (it must be raining!) and bring home **less** than two bags of loot (the second bag isn't full).

were not as advanced as the Britons had become under the Romans. And they were pagan, worshipping a host of Scandinavian gods of war and nature. In the last years of the Roman occupation, Rome had adopted Christianity, and the new faith had swept through Britain as well.

At first, the Britons and the new arrivals got along fairly peacefully, despite their differences. But then more and more immigrants came flooding in – Angles, Saxons, Jutes, and others – and began spreading through the southeast. The Britons fought many desperate battles, trying to drive the invaders out, but they failed.

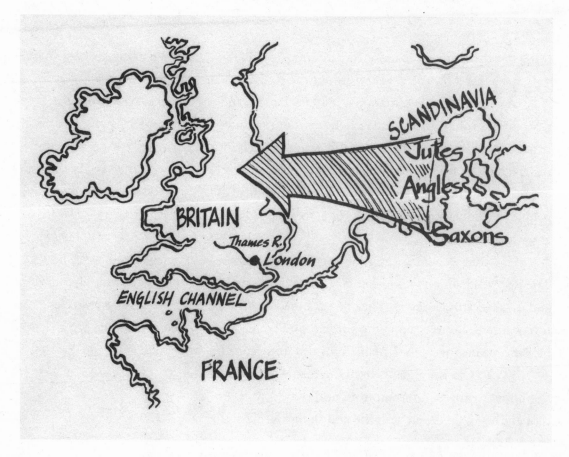

Although the borders of Anglo-Saxon Britain were constantly changing, we generally divide it into seven kingdoms: Essex, Wessex, Sussex, Kent, Mercia, Northumbria, and East Anglia.

By the mid-600s, there were Germanic communities through much of southern and eastern Britain. These grew into little kingdoms that were constantly fighting one another, killing each others' kings, merging territories and then splitting them up again. We call these people the Anglo-Saxons. They called themselves Angles, and their land was Engla-land. Their Germanic dialects, mixed with Celtic and Latin, became the early form of English we call Old English.

As the Anglo-Saxons took over, many Celts fled back across the sea to Europe, or deeper into the hinterlands of the west and south. The Anglo-Saxons dismissed them as foreigners, Wealas – the root of our word **Welsh**. (To this day Wales and Cornwall, in the far southwest, are strongholds of Celtic history and language.) The Wealas built tiny chapels and erected stone crosses, and clung to their Christianity. But while their faith remained strong, their memory of Latin slipped away. They repeated the rites and ceremonies of their church, but many of them barely understood the words they were saying.

The years after the fall of Rome are sometimes called the Dark Ages, because so much knowledge was lost, or at least temporarily misplaced. As the Roman Empire disintegrated into small territories, learning and culture took a back seat to rivalry and war. But Europe still had some important centers of scholarship, mostly in religious communities – especially in Rome, where the Catholic Church had grown wealthy and powerful.

In 597, the pope sent a party of monks, led by a learned monk named Augustine, to King Ethelbert of Kent, who was married to a Christian. Augustine persuaded Ethelbert to become Christian, and the religion began to spread through the Anglo-Saxon kingdoms. The monks built a church and monastery in Ethelbert's capital city, Canterbury. Augustine became the first Bishop of Canterbury, and later Saint Augustine of Canterbury. (Today, the Archbishop of Canterbury is still the senior clergyman of the Church of England.)

At first, many Anglo-Saxons resisted Christianity

fiercely. Monks and nuns were murdered; churches were robbed and burned. But the upper classes were gradually converted by scholars like Augustine, while country folk were won over by humble traveling priests. The pagan gods were set aside. The spring festival of the pagan goddess Eastre became Easter, and the pagan winter festival became the Christ-mass.

By the end of the 600s, most of England was once again Christian. New churches were built, and adorned with "ivories and jewelled crucifixes, golden and silver candelabra . . . superbly embroidered vestments, stoles and altar-cloths." Convents and monasteries sprang up, where ordinary people, as well as monks and nuns, could learn to read and write. The spread of literacy brought back basics of society like record-keeping and accounting and report-writing.

Meanwhile, the Anglo-Saxon kings were still fighting for supremacy. By the late 700s, King Offa of Mercia had more or less taken control of all the kingdoms, by various means (such as beheading the king of East Anglia). Offa called himself Rex Anglorum – Latin for "King of the English." But when he died in 796, his little empire fell apart. In the early 800s King Egbert of Wessex likewise managed, for a time, to control all the Anglo-Saxon domains, and he is sometimes counted as the first king of England.

But while the Anglo-Saxons continued their rivalry, some Scandinavian tribes to the east, across the sea, had plans of their own. By the late 700s, these bold Norsemen ("north-men," also called Vikings or Danes) were sailing to Britain and making fast, brutal raids – looting unprotected

These days, with scanners and photocopiers and faxes, it's hard to imagine the time and labor and mental concentration needed to reproduce a book by hand. Yet texts were not only copied meticulously, but embellished with illustrated initials and ornamental borders, sometimes with real gold. Notice all the birds and animals lurking in this capital P. And what's that funny little face in the top left?

churches and monasteries of their gold and silver treasures, burning precious manuscripts, smashing tombs, plundering villages, stealing horses, and slaughtering people or seizing them as slaves. "'From the fury of the Norsemen,' prayed the peasants in their churches, 'good Lord, deliver us!'"

The Vikings (Danes) had learned to be the world's best shipbuilders and sailors, because the rough northern seas were often the only road between their villages. In the 800s and 900s they were not only raiding Britain and northern France, but building their own settlements there. Sometime around the year 1000, their square-sailed, dragon-headed longboats, powered by oarsmen, even traveled as far as North America.

Before long, the Danes were not only raiding and going home again. They were beginning to take over the country for themselves – just as the Anglo-Saxons had done a few centuries earlier. Year after year the Vikings attacked Britain's coasts, and year after year they claimed more land as their own. Sometimes the Anglo-Saxons bribed them to go away, with payments called Danegeld (Danes' gold) – but sooner or later they always came back.

In 851, a fleet of Viking dragon boats moored in the Thames River, and the raiders burned London and Canterbury. In 865 they crossed Northumbria, looting and burning; they seized the city of York, and destroyed the school and library. In 869 they murdered the ruler of East Anglia when he refused to give up Christianity. In 872 the King of Mercia abandoned his crown and fled to Europe.

Now only one Anglo-Saxon dominion stood against the Danes – Wessex. It was ruled by a young king named Alfred.

The religious life offered women a refuge from difficult circumstances. For a few it was also a rare chance for a professional career. Princess Hilda of Northumbria (614-80) became a Christian when she was thirteen, and took her vows as a nun twenty years later. Revered for her wisdom and piety, she founded a church and "double convent" (for both men and women) at Whitby, on a cliff overlooking the sea. Hilda is now a saint.

ALFRED AND THE VIKINGS

When Alfred became King of Wessex in 871, the Vikings (Norsemen) controlled all of England north of the Thames – including the city of London – and they were attacking Wessex. Unable to defeat them right away, the new king played for time, paying a large bribe of Danegeld in exchange for a few years' peace. Meanwhile, he started building a fleet of warships to fight off the raiders. By 878 his army was able to win a decisive victory, and England was divided into Alfred's kingdom, and a region to the north and east (called the Danelaw) that was still held by the Norse.

Alfred trained and equipped a strong army to defend the kingdom, and fortified many of the towns. He took back London, and rebuilt it. He compiled a code of laws, reformed the justice system, and reorganized finances. He built monasteries and convents, and brought in foreign scholars to make the Church once again a center of learning.

He even invented some handy household gadgets, including a candle-lantern "clock" that measured time by the burning-speed of specially made candles. While he was doing all this, he was also fending off fresh attacks by the Vikings (Norse).

At the age of forty he learned Latin, and began translating important writings – including some by Saint Augustine – into Old English. Before then, English had been used for practical purposes like record-keeping and law-writing, and for poetry, but almost everything else was in Latin. Now, both translations and new works began to appear in Old English – Englisc, as it was called then.

Alfred the Great (849-899) is remembered as much for his wisdom and scholarship as for his political and military feats. "There will be more wisdom," he wrote, "the more languages we know."

> The Old English verb *witan* meaning "know" has fallen out of use, but it still casts a shadow. Today **wit** means cleverness or intelligence. **Unwittingly** means without knowing ("He unwittingly revealed the secret.") **Wise** people, **witnesses**, and **witches** and **wizards** are all named for their knowledge.

There were further clashes between the English and the Norse after Alfred's death in 899. In 1012, the Archbishop of Canterbury was slaughtered by drunken Vikings. For a short while, from 1016 to 1042, Norse kings once again ruled much of England. But Alfred was the turning point. He brought the Anglo-Saxons together, restored Christianity, and showed his people that they could be one great nation, with a language and literature of their own. For all of this, history remembers him as Alfred the Great.

Many of our most basic day-to-day words – **land**, **cow**, **sheep**, **dog**, **plow**, **bread** – come from Old English. **This** and **that** come from *this* and *thaet*. Our comparisons of **long**, **longer**, **longest** come from Old English *lang*, *lengra*, *lengest*. But as many of the invaders adopted Christianity, and the two peoples lived together and intermarried, their language – Old Norse – affected Old English. About seven percent of our words – **take**, **get**, and **keep**; **sky**, **skin**, and **skirt** – come from the Vikings. **He** is from Old English, but **they** is from Old Norse.

Etheldrida was a princess of East Anglia. As a girl she loved to wear fancy necklaces, but later she became deeply religious. When she developed a tumor on her neck, she saw it as God's punishment for her youthful vanity. After her death she became Saint Audrey, and the cheap, badly made lace sold in her honor – "Saint Audrey's lace" – gave us our word **tawdry** (t'audrey), meaning gaudy but worthless.

As Norse words passed into English, people could choose between an English-based term and a Norse-based one: **wish** or **want**, **craft** or **skill**, **hide** or **skin**. Over time, those similar words picked up slightly different meanings, different associations, and the English language grew more subtle and versatile. We still have distinctions like this, even if we don't think about them. For example, **Nativity** and **Yule** both mean "Christmas" – but **Nativity** ("birth," from a Latin root) suggests the religious side of the season, while **Yule** – from Old Norse *jol*, a twelve-day pagan festival – suggests a jolly good party. (Yes, **jolly** is also from *jol*.)

Old English nouns and pronouns varied depending on their case, but the changes were not as complicated as they had been in Latin and Greek. In fact, many pronouns looked very similar to ours:

	MODERN	OLD ENGLISH	MODERN	OLD ENGLISH
SUBJECT	I	*ic*	we	*we*
POSSESSIVE	mine	*min*	our	*ure*
OBJECT	me	*me*	us	*us*

In Old Norse, *by* meant "town." Today, **bylaws** are town laws (such as parking laws), and town names like Grimsby, Whitby, and Rugby echo those long-ago Viking invasions.

Although these forms haven't changed much in the past thousand years, people still get confused about the cases of pronouns. **I** or **me**? **He and she**, or **him and her**? There's an easy trick that can help you keep them straight.

Are these sentences right or wrong?

Dad saw John and I.
Mom wants she and Chris to go.
Harry thinks Lily and us are right.
Kids like you and I know a lot!

If you're not sure (and here's the BIG SECRET), drop one of the people. Drop **John and**, **and Chris**, **Lily and** and **you and**. See how wrong they all sound now? So if you're ever not sure which pronoun to use, you can either stop and think about the case – is it the subject or the

Old English had some letters we don't have: ð (*th* as in "cloth"), þ (*th* as in "clothe"), and ƿ (a *w* sound). A and E joined together (Æ or æ) sounded like *a* in "cat."

object of the verb? – or you can try dropping that confusing other person!

But if Old English and Old Norse were both inflected, with words changing their form depending on how they were used, why don't we have all those endings in modern English? As the Norse and Anglo-Saxons struggled to understand each other, they probably gave up most of the pesky endings, just to save trouble.

After all, if you were talking to someone who didn't speak much English, would you say, "Might I trouble you to pass the salt?" Or "Pass the salt, please"?

8 RIDDLES, HYMNS, AND TALES OF BATTLE

Much of what we know about Anglo-Saxon times comes from Saint Bede, who wrote – by hand, of course – countless works of history, religion, medicine, astronomy, even poetry and grammar.

Bede was born about two hundred years before Alfred's reign, in the days when most prose was still written in Latin. Other works – poems, word games, and long, elaborate riddle-verses – were sometimes written in Old English. What creature shoots from the stomach and can "serve no master when unstrung"? What complains that "Everybody lifts me, grips me, and chops off my head"? (See end of chapter.) But most of these writings have been lost, and the ones that survive are often anonymous.

The earliest English poet we know by name was a man called Caedmon, who lived around 670. In those days, before TV or radio or even printed books, poets recited works by memory, to entertain and inspire their au-

When Bede (673-735) was just seven years old, he was sent to the northern monastery of Jarrow. He spent almost all his life there, studying in the monastery's library and filling it with his own books – including a history of the English people (in Latin) ever since the days of Julius Caesar. Because of his intelligence and tireless scholarship, he's often called the Venerable (much-revered) Bede.

CÆDMON

In 1898 a sandstone cross was erected at Whitby with this picture of Caedmon; notice the horses in the stable. (The image of Saint Hilda in Chapter 6 is from the same cross.)

diences. According to Bede, Caedmon was an uneducated stablehand at the abbey in Whitby. One night a vision came to him and he was suddenly able to make up a hymn praising the *weorc Wuldor-Faeder* ("work of the Glory-Father," meaning God). Caedmon remained in Whitby as a lay brother (not a monk), composing other works.

Although Old English looks hard to read, the sounds suggest modern English. Speaking of God, Caedmon says, *He aerest sceop eorthan bearnum heofon to hrofe.* Try reading that out loud (pronouncing *sc* as *sh*) and comparing it to this translation: "He first shaped for earth's bairns [children] heaven as a roof . . ." (The next thing God shaped, according to Caedmon, was *middangeard* – middle earth.)

The most famous Old English work is *Beowulf,* an epic poem of over three thousand lines celebrating the feats of a "prince of warriors," and his courage and honor. The story comes from the myths and history of Scandinavia, where the adventures are set. We don't know when or where the poem was first recited, but the version that has come down to us is from a manuscript more than a thousand years old.

Beowulf defeats a gruesome monster, Grendel, ripping off Grendel's arm with his bare hands. Grendel's mother later attacks Beowulf in vengeance, and Beowulf dives to the bottom of a haunted lake and slays her and cuts off her head. Beowulf becomes king, but many years later he has to defend his people against a fiery dragon. The dragon is defeated but Beowulf dies in the battle, and is mourned as a noble and beloved leader.

Like Caedmon's poem, *Beowulf* is built out of short

half-lines that build up into sentences. The lines are held together not by rhyme, which the English rarely used in those days, but by powerful rhythm and lots of alliteration (words beginning with the same sound). Try reading these phrases out loud, pausing at the break; imagine how dramatic they would have sounded to an audience sitting in a great hall lit only by a fire, surrounded by darkness.

Grendel gongan   Godes yrre baer . . .
(Grendel walked in, bearing God's ire [anger]) . . . .

on fagne flor   feond treddode . . .
(on the fine floor the fiend trod) . . . .

Late in Alfred's reign, once Old English had been established as a language for serious writing, some monks began compiling a historical record called *The Anglo-Saxon Chronicle*. They filled in past events from whatever sources they could find, and kept adding to the book as the years went by. Here's some of the description of the desperate, bloody year when Alfred became king:

871: Then King Æthered fought the troops of the [Viking] kings, and King Barsecg [of

Here's the opening of *Beowulf*, in Old English written around 1000. This manuscript – the only one surviving from ancient times – was badly damaged in a fire in 1731, before any copies had been made, so some bits have been lost forever. The word order differs from ours, but the beginning says, "Truly we have heard of the glory of the Spear Danes' kings [*cyninga*] in yore-days [*in gear-dagum*]." *Gar* is an old word for **spear**; the Danes are called *Gar dena*.

J.R.R. Tolkien was a professor of English with a special interest in early languages. When he wrote *Lord of the Rings* he borrowed words from Old English: an *orc* is a demon, an *ent* is a giant, and the name of Rohan's King Theoden means "ruler." As for the dread land of Mordor, *morthor* is Old English for "death, destruction"; it's the root of our word **murder**.

the Vikings] was killed; and Æthered's brother Alfred fought the troops of the Viking earls, . . . and many thousand were slain, and they were fighting until nightfall. About a fortnight later, King Æthered and Alfred his brother fought the invading force at Basing, and there the Vikings were victorious. Two months after that, King Æthered and Alfred his brother fought at Merton, and there was great slaughter on both sides, but the Vikings controlled the battlefield. . . . Over Easter, King Æthered died; he had ruled for five years. . . . Then Alfred son of Æthelwulf came to the throne of Wessex. About a month later, King Alfred fought with a small company against the whole Viking force. . . . In that year, nine great battles were fought against the invading Vikings in the kingdom south of the Thames. . . .

At last, English was the accepted language of prose and poetry, of science and history, of law-writing and account-keeping. Priests and scholars might still work in Latin and Greek, but English had finally won its place as the language of England.

Or so it seemed.

9

THE DEFEAT OF THE ENGLISH

England was not the only land invaded by the Vikings. During the 800s, the Norsemen had sent their dragon boats up the rivers of northern France, raiding and burning Paris and other cities. Then they had moved in and begun building settlements. In 911, to put an end to their raids, the French king had granted them land on the north coast of France. The Norse leader had converted to Christianity and had been made a duke. Now these Vikings were called Normans, their territory was Normandy, and they came to speak their own Norman version of French.

By 1042, England was ruled by a religious but weak king named Edward the Confessor. Edward was descended from Alfred the Great, but his mother was from Normandy and he had grown up in the Norman court. Many people in England thought he was much too friendly with the Normans. Apparently Edward even promised the English throne to their leader, William, Duke of Normandy, since Edward himself had no heir.

In 1064, a rich and powerful English nobleman – Harold, Earl of Wessex – was shipwrecked on the coast of Normandy. It seems that he vowed to support the duke's claim to the throne of England. (Harold may have been forced to make this promise.) But two years later, when Edward the Confessor died, it was Harold who took over the throne.

William of Normandy's victory is portrayed in the Bayeux Tapestry, an ancient strip of embroidered linen that is 230 feet (70m) long. The Latin shown here says, *Harold Rex Interfectus Est* — "King Harold is killed." According to legend, Harold was shot in the eye with an arrow, but experts aren't sure whether he's the victim on the left, or the one on the right — or both!

William of Normandy was furious. He loaded troops onto a fleet of ships and sailed for England, to claim the country for himself. The two armies met in battle near the town of Hastings in October 1066, shooting rafts of arrows, hurling spears, dueling face to face with swords, clubs, and battle-axes. The Normans probably had no more than five thousand soldiers, but they had one great advantage: their knights rode horses specially bred and trained for combat. The English used horses for transportation, but they had never before faced an enemy fighting from horseback.

By the end of the day King Harold was dead, and so were many of his noblemen. William of Normandy – who was clever and practical, but merciless – led his army across southern England and seized the city of London. On Christmas Day he was crowned England's new king – William the Conqueror.

The Normans expanded their power throughout England, building massive stone castles with moats and drawbridges, and manning them with soldiers. One by one, the English lords were killed or driven from their lands, and Norman barons took their place. Each baron had to keep a host of armed knights ready to do battle whenever the king needed them. Norman French was suddenly the language of law and government, the language of the ruling class, the language of fashionable literature.

When William of Normandy landed in England in 1066, he set up camp inside the walls of Anderida, a sea fort built by the Romans eight hundred years earlier to hold off the Vikings. After defeating King Harold, the Normans built Pevensey Castle on Anderida's remains, and used it for about two hundred years. Notice the mighty keep (refuge) at the back, and the twin towers of the gatehouse in front, where the bridge crosses the moat. In the 1500s, when Spain sent a vast "Armada" of warships against England, Pevensey was refortified to resist the attack. In World War II, machine-gun posts were hidden in Pevensey's walls in case of a German invasion.

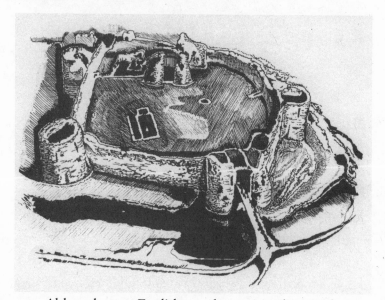

Although most English people continued to speak their own language, and Old English was still used for some writing, French words inevitably filtered into English – especially words connected with government or fine living. The English we speak today still has traces of the social gap between the victorious Normans and the conquered English. **Crown** is from French *couronne*; **parliament** is from French *parlement*; **royal** is from Old French *roial*. The cow and pig down in the stable are from Old English (*cu* and *pigga*); the beef and pork up in the dining hall are from Old French (*boef* and *porc*). Plain straw and wool: Old English *streaw* and *wull*; elegant lace and velvet: Old French *laz* and *veluotte*. Most English words ending in *ion*, *or*, *ment*, or *ence* (like **mention**, **honor**, **compliment**, or **patience**) came from French.

We still use French (or French-based) expressions to sound sophisticated. It's *chic* to have good *etiquette*, to be *debonair* (with a *bon aire*, "good air") and *nonchalant* (not *chalé*, worried). We'd like enough *savoir-faire* to know how to behave, enough *savoir-vivre* to know how to enjoy life, and enough *sang-froid* (cool blood) to stay calm in the face of danger. The French even have a name for what they can't name – it's a *je ne sais quoi* ("I don't know what").

> Back in the 1890s, only a few rich people had cars, and it took a while to get them going. The employee who was sent out ahead of time, to *chauffer* (warm up) the engine so it would run properly, was called a **chauffeur**.

And look how French dominates fine dining! At a *restaurant* or *café* we are greeted by the *maître d'* and we order a *gourmet* dinner *à la carte* – an *apéritif*, *pâté*, or cheese *soufflé* as an *hors d'oeuvre*. "And for the *entrée*, the *chef* suggests the *quiche* or *fondue*, or a *casserole*. And then perhaps some *éclairs*, *meringue*, *sorbet*, *crème brûlée*?"

The Norman Conquest also brought more Latin into English. Although Latin was still used in church, it had pretty much disappeared from England's daily life after the Romans went home. But French had grown from Latin, and now Latin roots (and Latin ways of organizing a sentence) were back, buried in Norman French. On top of that, much of the history and record-keeping that had been done in English was switched back to Latin. After 1154, there are no more entries in the *Anglo-Saxon Chronicle*. One in three words in English today comes from Latin – directly from the Romans, or through the church, or through the Normans, or through more modern French.

· ·

Which is correct — "one in three *is*" or "one in three *are*"? This looks confusing because "three" is closer to the verb — don't we say "three *are*"? But it's the actual subject of the verb that has to match the verb. That subject is "one" — "in three" describes it but doesn't change the number — so we say "<u>one in three</u> is," just as we'd say "the <u>one in trouble</u> is." When people let a subject and verb disagree in number, it's often because something in between confused them. They say, "Each of the **lions have their** own den" — *each have?* What they should say is "**Each** of the lions **has its** own den." They say, "The turtle is one of the oldest animals that lives in the zoo" — *animals that lives?* "The turtle is one of the oldest animals that **live** in the zoo" is correct.

Just remember whether the subject of your sentence is singular or plural, and make the verb match. Simple!

English had already lost some of its complications in the days when the Anglo-Saxons and Vikings were trying to understand each other. Now, as English people tried to cope with Norman French and Latin as well, their language lost yet more of its endings, and became even simpler. And once again, as foreign words slipped into the vocabulary, English became more subtle and versatile at expressing different shades of meaning.

The Norman Conquest of 1066 turned out to be another of history's great turning points, and its effect lives on in both Britain and the English language. Next time you see a picture of handsome young Prince William, grandson of Queen Elizabeth II and likely a future king, remember that one of his ancestors is William the Conqueror, that heir to the Vikings, who crossed the Channel to seize England's throne almost a thousand years ago.

"How stinky! Well, not stinky, exactly, but . . . ." We're lucky that English gives us so many ways to say what we mean. When we can't think of exactly the right word, we can reach for a thesaurus — which sounds like some kind of dinosaur, but is really a book of words grouped by general meaning (*thesauros* is Greek for **treasure**). If you look up **stink** in the index of one popular thesaurus, you're directed to a section labeled **Fetor** — which offers choices like **stench, rank, rancid, musty, fusty, skunky, fetid, putrid,** and (oddly!) **garlic**. The thesaurus is a handy tool when you're writing, but remember: all these words have slightly different senses. It's up to you to decide which one is just right.

10

Crusaders brought home stories of distant lands and exotic beasts. Fire-breathing dragons were a popular feature, especially if they were guarding fair maidens or fabulous treasures. Beowulf had killed a dragon, after all, and so had Saint George, England's patron saint. Since Christians often portrayed dragons as symbols of the Devil, killing them was noble and virtuous.

The Norman Conquest of 1066 was followed by years of unrest, chaos, even civil war. King after king struggled to crush rebellions in England, and to subdue the Welsh, Scots, and Irish. Being as ambitious and warlike as their Viking ancestors, the Norman kings were also fighting to win more territory in France.

When they weren't doing battle with the French, the Norman English were riding beside them as allies on religious crusades – military campaigns to take back Palestine, the Holy Land of Christians, Jews, and Muslims, from the Muslims. Throughout the 1100s and 1200s, kings, noblemen, and knights rode off to seek victory in the Middle East. Often they stayed away for years. Richard Lion-Heart (the king in the Robin Hood story) ruled England for ten years but spent only six months in the country; most of the time he was away on a crusade.

The Holy Land wasn't the only place the Europeans

wanted to reclaim. Back in 711 – in the days of the Anglo-Saxon kingdoms, before the Vikings began their raids – an Arab army had crossed the Mediterranean from Africa and seized much of Spain. It took the Europeans hundreds of years to drive the Muslims out.

With all this warfare between Arabs and Europeans, there was a constant exchange of ideas and language, and many Arab words were transformed into English – like *suffah* (sofa), *sukkar* (sugar), *ghul* (ghoul), and *makhazin* (magazine). A *matrah* was a place where you put down your mattress; your *rahat* was the palm of your hand, which holds your tennis racket; an orange was a *naranj*.

Notice how the *n* of *naranj* drifted off the noun and attached itself to the indefinite article, **a.** Sounds often floated one way or the other, back in the days when most people couldn't read or write, and just repeated whatever they thought they'd heard. **An apron** used to be **a napron** (**napron** is related to **napkin**); a newt was **an ewt**; **a nick-name** was **an ekename** (eke meant "extra"); **an umpire** was **a noumpere**, a "non-peer" rather than one of the players.

Long ago, alchemy was the search for a way to turn cheap metals into silver and gold. The unknown liquid that would make this happen was called **the elixir** (from the Arabic *al-iksir; al* is Arabic for "the"). **Alchemy** and **chemistry** are from the Arabic word *al-kimiya,* "the art of transforming metals." These days an elixir is a medicine, perhaps one promised to cure all ills and help you live forever.

Why are some verbs so easy — **I walk, I walked, I have walked** — and some so bizarre? Look at **eat ate eaten, freeze froze frozen, slay slew slain, see saw seen, sing sang sung.** Verbs that have different forms for the past tense come from the Scandinavian roots of English, not Latin or French. There used to be about three hundred and fifty of them, but many have gradually lost their irregular forms. Of the sixty or so odd verbs that remain, some are half gone. You'll hear people say, "She sung" instead of "She sang," or "I rung the bell" instead of "I rang."

Old English was now evolving into Middle English (spoken from 1100 to 1500, more or less). Most nouns started taking an *s* in the plural, though a few continued to change their vowel (**goose/geese**) or to take an *en* ending (**ox/oxen**), or didn't change at all (**fish/fish**). Endings that showed the case of a noun were being replaced by prepositions: **of, to, from,** and so on. Letters like *ð, þ* and *æ* gradually disappeared. Words like *cnawan* and *cniht* (**know** and **knight**) traded their *c* for a *k*, and in time the *k* became silent. Many of our silent letters today — the *g* in **gnaw**, the *l* in **would** — are whispers of letters that were pronounced in those days.

Literature was changing too. The Normans brought French styles of poetry to England – including *chansons de geste* ("songs of deeds") that celebrated the adventures of gallant, gentlemanly knights who risked death to please God (or some fair lady). Though the first *chansons* were in French, some were soon translated for those who spoke only English, and then original English works began to appear.

The most famous writer of the time is Geoffrey Chaucer. His best-known work, *The Canterbury Tales*, tells of a group of people "high and low, old and young, male and female, lay and clerical, learned and ignorant, rogue and righteous, land and sea, town and country," riding to Canterbury together on a religious pilgrimage, and passing the time by telling stories. Chaucer includes humorous details about each of the travelers — merchant, miller, housewife, nun — and each story imitates that traveler's own speech, painting us a picture of how these people would have "cursed and complained and questioned and told each other jokes," six hundred years ago. Unlike Caedmon's hymn, this poem depends more on rhyme than on alliteration. Here's how he introduces a "parfit gentil knight." (To make the rhythm work, pronounce the underlined letters as extra syllables.)

Many romantic poems were about King Arthur and his Knights of the Round Table, and his court at Camelot. (Arthur had, of course, killed a dragon.) Although his story is still being told in books, songs, plays, and movies, Arthur remains a mystery. Was he real? Or is his story just a myth?

> A Knight ther was, and that a worthy man,
> That fro the tim<u>e</u> that he first bigan
> To riden out, he lov<u>ed</u> chivalrye,
> Trouth<u>e</u> and honour, freedom and curteisye.

Chaucer started this poem in 1386, but we don't know exactly how he wrote it, because the manuscripts from his time (written by hand) have been lost. All we have now are later copies.

As a youth, Chaucer (1340?-1400) served as a pageboy to royalty, and learned courtly manners as well as Latin and French. Later, as a diplomat and civil servant, he was sent to France and Italy. His writings are rich in words, ideas, and story twists that he brought back from his travels. Unlike the dragon-slaying heroes in tales of chivalry, his characters are as real and down to earth as anyone you might meet on the road.

But here's another poem – an anonymous work called "I Have a Young Sister" – that shows us what English looked like around 1300. It's similar to the riddle-verses the Anglo-Saxons wrote hundreds of years earlier. The poet announces that his young sister has sent him a cherry with no stone and a dove with no bones.

> How sholde any cherye
> > Be withoute stoon?
> And how sholde any dove
> > Be withoute boon? . . .
>
> Whan the cherye was a flowr,
> > Thanne hadde it no stoon;
> Whan the dove was an ey [egg],
> > Thanne hadde it no boon.

What did the poet's sister send him? (If you find this hard to understand, try reading it out loud. There's a modern version at the end of the chapter.)

English was flourishing in all kinds of ways. Although the aristocrats still spoke French and boasted of their French blood, they had to speak English to their servants, their staff, and the farmers on their estates. By the 1300s, Parliamentary proceedings were again conducted in English. By 1350, English had replaced Latin as the teaching language in most schools. In 1362, English replaced French in the law courts, although legal records were still in Latin. In 1399, Henry IV became the first king since the 1066 Norman Conquest to make his coronation speech in

English. The offficials of the kingdom followed his example, doing more and more of their work in English.

By the mid-1400s, the Normans had lost almost all their territory in France. They had become English, and anglophone (English-speaking), whether they liked it or not. English was once again the language of the land.

Modern version of "I Have a Young Sister"
How could a cherry not have a stone [pit]?
And how could a dove not have any bones? . . .
When the cherry was a flower, it had no stone;
When the dove was an egg, it had no bones.

One reason for the decline of Latin was the Black Death, a terrible epidemic of bubonic plague that reached England in 1348. Spread by fleas on the rats that infested wooden merchant ships, the disease killed thirty to forty percent of England's population. By the time that wave of plague was over, there weren't enough teachers left to educate children in French, let alone Latin, so most schools taught in English. The plague would flare up again and again in the centuries to come.

11

HOW TO SPELL IT? HOW TO SAY IT?

While fewer people were learning French and Latin, more were learning to read and write English. The old cathedral schools staffed by monks and priests had grown into universities. (Oxford and Cambridge – probably the most famous universities in the world – both date back to the 1200s.) Smaller schools and private tutors were much in demand. But there was one huge problem: creating a book still meant writing it out by hand. One hard-working scribe – often a monk or nun in a writing hall called a scriptorium – might complete as little as a hundred pages in a year. So books remained expensive, and most people couldn't afford them.

But all that was about to change. In the 1400s, a few people in Europe realized that if they molded little letters backwards – A ꓭ Ɔ – and grouped them into a block of words, they could create the reverse image of a page. Then the block could be covered with ink and pressed against paper to make a real page. (People in China and Korea had been doing this for years, but it seems the Europeans hadn't heard about it.) After the individual letters (called movable type) had been used to print enough copies of that page, they could be taken apart and assembled differently to spell out another page, and another.

A scribe works on the laborious process of copying a book, in the early 1500s. (**Scribe** is from Latin *scribo,* "I write.")

In 1455, a German named Johannes Gutenberg printed a Bible in Latin, using movable type. Copies were soon on sale across England and Europe. Then an Englishman named William Caxton went to Germany to learn the procedure, and created the first English book

A page from Chaucer's *Canterbury Tales*, in Caxton's version of 1484, with an illustration of the "parfit gentil knight." Caxton (1422-1491) printed over ninety books in all, seventy-four of them in English. It troubled him that the handwritten books he copied could be full of mistakes, but he took pains to work from the most accurate, most original text he could lay hands on.

ever printed. Around 1476, Caxton went back to England, built himself a wooden printing press, and went to work. He produced books of his own writings, and translations of foreign writings (including Aesop's fables), and Chaucer's *Canterbury Tales,* and *Le Morte D'Arthur*, a long English-language account of King Arthur and his knights.

One of the problems Caxton had to resolve was how to spell the works he translated. He wanted his books to be read all across England, but different regions pronounced and spelled words differently, and even used different words for the same thing. Which version should he choose? To explain his difficulty, Caxton told the story of a hungry traveler who asked a countrywoman for *egges*. She had no idea what the word meant. Then another man asked her for *eyren*, and she gave him – eggs. "Loo," wondered Caxton, "what sholde a man in thyse dayes now wryte, egges or eyren?" After much consideration, he decided to reproduce (more or less) the words and spellings used by officials in London. After all, their English was similar to the English used at Oxford and Cambridge. How could it be wrong?

Books printed before 1501 – when printing was still in its infancy – are extremely rare and precious. They're known as **incunabula**, Latin for "baby's cradle."

Now that publishing was so much faster and cheaper, a snowstorm of books, pamphlets, and other writings swept across the country. In 1525, the first English translation of the Bible's New Testament was printed. A complete English Bible was published ten years later, another version in 1537, and two more in 1539. By this time, perhaps half the population could read, and books (especially the Bible) were becoming part of their daily life. The words and spellings chosen by Caxton and other printers became the normal, customary forms. Eggs were *egges*, and if you called them *eyren*, well, you must be ignorant.

In Caxton's day, many scholarly books were still in Latin. But soon, more and more were printed in English. As late as 1653, *Grammatica Linguae Anglicanae* – a book explaining the grammar of the English language – was written in Latin. But by the late 1600s, even the most important academic and scientific works were being published in English. And as scholars used English to explore all areas of human thought, no matter how complex, their vocabulary had to expand. Now, English had to have the power and precision of classical Latin and Greek.

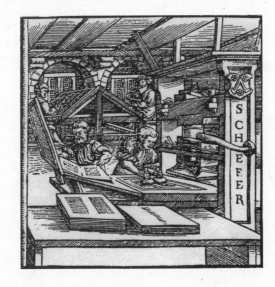

A printing shop in the early 1500s. Workers at the back are assembling letters of backwards type into a page-size block. Those at the front are rubbing ink onto the page block, and pressing sheets of blank paper against the block to print a stack of pages. Our expression "the press," meaning newspapers and magazines, comes from this pressing of paper against inky type.

Meanwhile, something very strange was happening to speech – something known as the "great vowel shift." Starting around 1400, people changed the way they pronounced certain vowels.

We have five real vowels (*a*, *e*, *i*, *o*, and *u*), and *y*, which is sometimes a vowel and sometimes not. We have various ways of pronouncing them. They can be short (b<u>i</u>t, m<u>a</u>t) or long (b<u>i</u>te, m<u>a</u>te). They can be silent, or run together into a single sound (cr<u>ea</u>m), or one can slide into another (c<u>oi</u>n). Sometimes they stand side by side but we say them separately, as in N<u>oë</u>l. (The two dots over the *e* tell you that the vowels are pronounced separately.)

Many old words have fallen out of use, but some of them still pop up inside other words. *Tadde* used to mean "toad," and *pol* meant "head." (Today, a **poll** is a count of one vote per person – one vote per *head*.) A toad that was mostly head – that wiggly, legless larva that grows into a toad or frog – used to be a *taddepol* ("toad-head"). That's why we call it a **tadpole**.

Do you say *tomayto* or *tomahto*? Do you call pigeons *brrds*, *bards*, *beds*, *buhds*, or *boyds*? The way we pronounce vowels varies from place to place, and even from person to person. In the movie *My Fair Lady*, Eliza, a ragged flower-seller who's learning to talk like a fine lady, has to work desperately hard to say that rain in Spain (not *rine in Spine*) falls mainly on the plain (not *minely on the pline*).

Pronunciation also changes over time. In Chaucer's

day, **fine** rhymed with **bean**; **see** rhymed with **say**; **to** rhymed with **no**. But in the great vowel shift, many long vowels changed dramatically, to the pronunciations we use today. That's one reason why old poetry like Chaucer's sometimes doesn't seem to rhyme.

Have you ever wondered why **police** and **polite** don't have the same *i*-sound? It's because **polite** is an old word, and the sound of the *i* changed during the great vowel shift. **Police** came into English after the shift, so it never changed.

As for spelling, while some people find it difficult, there are tricks to make it easier. If you think about what the word means, what other words it resembles, and what language it comes from, you are more likely to remember the spelling. For example, *terra* is Latin for **earth**, **land**, **ground**. If you can spell **terrier** (a dog that burrows into the ground), you know how many *r*s there are in **subterranean** (underground), **Mediterranean** (a sea in the middle of the land), **terrestrial** (on earth), **terraforming** (transforming another planet to resemble earth), and so on.

Kids who compete in spelling bees (contests) have an amazing ability to remember how thousands of words are spelled. When the judge asks them to spell a word, they're allowed to ask what the word means; if it sounds like "tericolous" (with one *r*) but it means "living on the earth," they can guess that it's **terricolous**, from *terra*. They can ask what part of speech the word is (noun? verb?); the noun **callus** (a hard spot on skin) is spelled differently from the adjective **callous**. They can ask what language it comes from; a word that sounds like Latin *terra* might actually come from Greek *pteron*, "wing," with that tricky silent *p*.

Which is right: "a historic moment" or "an historic moment"? "A herb" or "an herb"? Some people omit the *h* ("aitch") on these words, so they need "an" as the indefinite article ("an 'istoric," "an 'erb") – but if you pronounce the aitch, drop the *n* ("a historic," "a herb"). Poor Eliza struggles to pronounce her aitches in *My Fair Lady*, huffing them into a flame – "<u>h</u>urricanes <u>h</u>ardly <u>h</u>appen" – to make it flicker.

Two good movies show what a spelling bee is like. *Akeelah and the Bee* tells a story about a girl who loves to spell and ends up in a bee. *Spellbound* follows a real-life spelling bee as, one after another, contestants flub their words, until only the winner is left. Both movies show how much training and practice and hard work it takes to be a winner – and how scary it is to be up on that stage, spelling words you've never even heard of.

Many people have argued that we should simplify our spelling, and write words the way they sound. But others treasure our weird spellings as a mini-history of the English language. These seemingly strange words are an echo of all those long-ago voices, from so many different cultures and places, that left their mark on this language called English.

Can you guess the spelling of these words from their sound?
They are all tough to figure out, but words like this (and harder) show up in
spelling bees. See how close you can come, using the clues you're given.

	sounds like	language of origin	part of speech	meaning
1.	KREEGspeel	German	noun	a game based on warfare
2.	laKUStreen	Latin	adjective	concerning lakes
3.	seFOlojy	Greek	noun	the study of elections
4.	booyaBESS	French	noun	fish stew
5.	zabelYOnee	Italian	noun	custardy dessert

ANSWERS

SPELLING-BEE ANSWERS:

1. **Kriegspiel.** In German, the letter *k* is fairly common and *ie* is pronounced "*ee*," as in **wiener**.

2. **Lacustrine.** Latin rarely uses the letter *k*, and *ine* is a common spelling for an adjective's ending, though it's pronounced various ways: pristine, feminine, canine.

3. **Psephology.** Both *ps* and *ph* are single letters in Greek so these combinations appear often, and a word ending in *ology* usually means some field of study.

4. **Bouillabaisse.** The *ill* combination is pronounced *y* in French, and if the ending had a single *s* it would be pronounced "bez" instead of "bess."

5. **Zabaglione.** The letter *z* is more common in Italian than in English, and *gli* is pronounced *lyi.* Many Italian words end in a soft *e* sound.

12

MAKING THE "GOOD BOOK" BETTER

I n the early days of printing, England was still a Catholic country. It's difficult now to imagine the power that the Church (and the Pope in Rome) had back then, before science improved our lives and helped us understand the world around us. The winters were long and cold, and the typical house was a bare, dark, drafty hut with no heating but a fire. There were few remedies for small miseries like fleas and lice, or aches and pains. Once autumn was past, most people had to survive on whatever food could be dried or salted. When illness or disaster struck, it seemed to come out of nowhere, for no earthly reason.

But churches, abbeys, and cathedrals, with their lofty pillars and soaring spires, lifted people out of all this. Altars glittered with treasures of silver and gold. Massive stonework echoed the music from organs, choirs, and pealing bells. Statues and paintings and stained-glass windows told stories of virtue triumphant. Feasts and pageants and processions broke up the weary work year. There was drama; there was mystery; above all, there was the promise that those who obeyed God's will during their lifetime would enjoy a glorious eternity.

The church was the center of the community, consoling people for hard times and giving them hope for the future. Overflowing with beauty, glowing with color, it was an earthly promise of heavenly joy.

The cloak (*cappa* in Latin) of Saint Martin of Tours, who lived in the 300s, was preserved in a church in a special shrine called the *cappella*. In time, any small area dedicated to worship became known as a *cappella*, or **chapel**. (*Cappella* is also connected to **cobra**, the snake that looks as if it's wearing a hood.)

People depended on priests to tell them what it was God wanted, and to help them atone for any sins they committed, so they could avoid eternal damnation. Most Bibles and other religious books were still in Latin, and church services were conducted in Latin, even though the congregation didn't understand the language. Indeed, a lot of country priests didn't know much Latin, especially after so many perished in the Black Death. They just followed the rites and rituals they had been taught.

But the immense wealth and influence of the Church led to problems. One was the conflict between the power of local rulers and the decrees of Church authorities. The Church even decided which books people could read and which were forbidden. Another problem was corruption. While many priests were faithful to their duties, some – especially high-ranking officials – lived in pomp and luxury, and abused their position to fill their pockets. Among other things, they sold indulgences – free pardons – that let rich people "buy forgiveness" for bad behavior.

Back in the 1300s some people had called for reform, saying that the Church's wealth should be put to better use, and that common people should be able to read the Bible for themselves. But while the Bible had been translated into English, at that time it still had to be copied by hand, and there weren't enough books to go around.

By the 1500s, though, the protest movement was growing stronger. Those protesting – the "Protestants" – wanted everyone to have access to the Bible. They argued that people should learn to live by their own judgment and conscience, and find salvation through their personal faith – not through favors bought from the Church.

And then along came printing, and the Church no longer controlled the Bible.

In 1525 that first English printing of the New Testa-

When the Church approved a book for publication, it decreed, *"Imprimatur"* – Latin for "Let it be printed." Today, **imprimatur** means any official approval – "The new dog park bylaws have the mayor's imprimatur."

ment appeared, translated and printed by an English priest named William Tyndale. Church officials opposed Tyndale, knowing that he supported the protest movement. In any case, it was considered heresy (a crime against God) to translate the Bible into English without permission. Tyndale had to print his Bibles in Europe and smuggle them into England, hidden in bales of cloth and other wares. When copies were found, they were seized and tossed into a fire. People who had them were imprisoned, even tortured and burned alive – just for daring to own a Bible.

But the Church soon had something new to worry about. King Henry VIII was desperate for a son who could inherit his throne. (After all, no woman could be trusted to rule England!) He wanted to end his marriage and take a new, younger wife. The Pope refused to let him do it.

In 1534, Henry broke away from the Roman Catholic Church and declared himself head of a new Church of England (the Anglican Church). He closed Catholic monasteries, destroyed shrines, and took over the lands and treasures of the old churches. People who got in Henry's way found their heads on the chopping-block. Enough of this interference from Rome; the English monarch was now the leader of the English church.

With Rome out of the picture, a number of English-language Bibles were soon on the market. In 1539, a "Great Bible" was published under Henry's authority. People across England were reading their Bibles and other books about religion, and asking questions, and making up their own minds about God and their faith. Biblical phrases were becoming everyday expressions: "my brother's

Tyndale (1494?-1536) was an exceptional scholar, reading Spanish, Italian, German, and Hebrew as well as English, French, Latin, and Greek, but he paid dearly for his beliefs. He went into hiding in Europe and kept on translating, but English authorities tracked him down and arrested him. He was tied to a cross and strangled, and his body was burned.

keeper," "the writing on the wall," "an eye for an eye," "casting pearls before swine."

As for Henry VIII, he did finally get a son, but the boy-king died just six years after Henry's death in 1547. Henry's older daughter, Mary, who had remained a devout Catholic, became queen and married King Philip of Spain. In the fifty-odd years since Christopher Columbus had found America in 1492, Spanish armies had defeated and ransacked the empires of the Aztecs in Mexico and the Incas farther south. Shiploads of gold, silver, and gems from America had made Spain immensely wealthy, and a powerful ally for England.

In her determination to turn England Catholic again, Queen Mary (1516-1568) persecuted Protestants and had almost three hundred people burned at the stake, including the Archbishop of Canterbury. She's remembered as Bloody Mary.

But Mary died after only five years on the throne. Her successor – Henry's second daughter, Elizabeth – would reign for forty-five years. Although religious conflict continued through much of that time, Elizabeth was firmly Anglican, and England remained Anglican too.

By the time of Elizabeth's successor, James I, Church authorities felt there were too many different Bibles around; they wanted a new official version. Some fifty

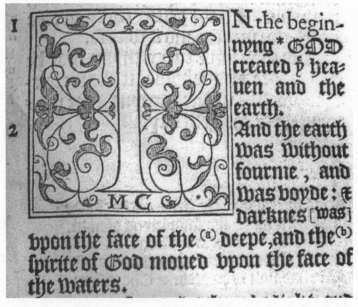

Bishops of the Anglican Church disapproved of some of the attitudes expressed in various Bibles. In 1568 they published their own version, the "Bishops' Bible," and made it the official Bible of the Anglican Church. (The word "bible" comes from Greek *biblos*, "scroll" or "book" – also the root of **bibliophile**, "book-lover.") Here's the beginning of the Book of Genesis, opening with a decorative initial: *In the beginning God created the heaven and the earth. And the earth was without form, and was void, and darkness was upon the face of the deep, and the spirit of God moved upon the face of the waters.* In the third line, "the" has been shortened to y^e. In the second-last line, "spirit" begins with a long form of *s*, like an *f* with one arm missing.

Do you notice something funny about these personal pronouns?

	LATIN	OLD ENGLISH	BIBLE	FRENCH	ENGLISH
SINGULAR					
subject	tu	thu	thou	tu	you
object	te	the	thee	te	you
PLURAL					
subject	vos	ge	you	vous	you
object	vos	eow	you	vous	you

What happened to all those other forms? Why do we always use **you**?

In many languages, the singular form is considered informal – all right for talking to children or friends, but not for strangers or people senior to you. In Chaucer's time, the land-owner called the peasant "thou" but the peasant respectfully called the land-owner "you." (The French have a word for this; to call people *tu* is to *tutoyer* them.) But as the gap between classes shrank, people began calling everyone "you" to avoid labeling one person as inferior to another.

If the distinction seems odd, consider this: we call children and friends by their first names ("Hey, Chris!") but we often use last names to show respect for other people ("Hi, Mrs. Jacobs"). Back when rich people had lots of servants, they might call the maid "Alice" but they called the cook "Mrs." even if she wasn't married. Servant or not, they had to treat her with respect if they valued their dinner!

scholars worked for several years, revising and retranslating, and depending greatly on William Tyndale's work a hundred years earlier. Their goal was to produce a Bible that was beautifully written, yet accurate and easy to understand. If a passage described carpentry, they asked carpenters what words to use; if trees were the subject, they consulted gardeners.

Try reading this speech of Ruth's out loud, listening to the flow of the language. (Ruth's husband has died, and her mother-in-law has said that Ruth should go back to her own people.)

> Intreat me not to leave thee, or to return
> from following after thee: for whither thou
> goest, I will go; and where thou lodgest, I
> will lodge: thy people shall be my people,
> and thy God my God. . . .

13

GLORIANA AND THE BARD

When the English weren't cutting off people's heads, they were hanging them, especially from the dreaded gallows on Tyburn Hill, near London. Big cranes called **derricks**, used to hoist cargo onto ships, take their name from a Mr. Derrick, a hangman who "hoisted" convicts there some four hundred years ago.

When Elizabeth Tudor was still a toddler, her father, Henry VIII, had her mother's head cut off. Being Anglican, Elizabeth was lucky not to lose her own head in the years when her Catholic half-sister, Queen Mary, was trying to lead England back to the "true" faith.

When Mary died and Elizabeth became queen, she found her new realm in sad shape. England was weak and nearly bankrupt, torn by religious violence, riddled with crime, and threatened by richer and stronger Catholic neighbors, France and Spain.

But Elizabeth was highly intelligent, well educated, and skilled in six languages. She was shrewd and practical, and too sensible to waste her resources on war if she could possibly avoid it. During her long reign, she fended off

Though she looks calm and confident, Elizabeth I (1533-1603) had to fight hard to keep her throne. One of the gravest dangers was her Catholic, half-French cousin, Mary, Queen of Scots (not to be confused with Elizabeth's half-sister, Bloody Mary), who kept plotting to take the throne, bring back Catholicism, and make England an ally of France. After years of protecting her troublesome cousin, Elizabeth reluctantly agreed to have Mary, Queen of Scots executed. But after Elizabeth died childless, it was Mary's son who ascended the English throne as James I – the Anglican who put his name on the King James Bible.

foreign attacks by dallying with at least fifteen marriage proposals. (Even the King of Spain – Queen Mary's widower – hoped to marry Elizabeth and recover England as an ally.) Along the way, Elizabeth almost died of smallpox, and ducked endless conspiracies to exploit her, kidnap her, even murder her.

To defend the country, Elizabeth made sure the army and the great navy her father had begun were rebuilt and modernized. While Europe was suffering terrible religious wars and atrocities, she did her best to create tolerance and cooperation among the English. The resulting peace and security brought a boom in trade and industry. Elizabeth symbolized a prosperous golden age, and her subjects

In Elizabeth's day, some writers felt they had to use classical languages if they wanted their thoughts preserved for eternity (which of course they did). But others deliberately wrote in English, borrowing from Greek and Latin when necessary, to make their own language as rich and versatile as any other. Indeed, some *detested* the remnants of Latin and Greek, and wanted them rooted out of the English language. One bishop argued that instead of calling something "penetrable" (from Latin *penetrare*), we should call it "gothroughsome" (from Old English *gan-thurh-sum*).

– many of them, at least – adored her. Gloriana, they called her. A few even built their homes in the shape of an E, to show their devotion.

Now that they had time and money to spend on themselves, many people turned to entertainment, especially plays. Small companies of actors sprang up. Before that, plays had been staged in any available space, but now real theaters were built, where even poor laborers could stand and watch for just a penny. (Whenever the plague returned, the theaters had to shut down for months or years, until it was over.) By 1592, one of the people working in London theater – acting, writing, perhaps directing – was William Shakespeare.

Shakespeare was a country boy, born in Stratford-on-Avon (*avon* is a Celtic word for **river**). We don't know much about his early life. His father was a leather-worker, and later a town official. Shakespeare seems to have had a reasonably good education, although he didn't go to university.

Like Chaucer, Shakespeare created lively characters of all types and classes who thought and talked just the way they should. Then he wove them into brilliant tales that felt true to life, no matter how far away or long ago they were set. Shakespeare's language is quite similar to what we speak today. There are some outdated words, and many references from that age of horse-carts and sailing ships are unfamiliar to us now. But for the most part, this is the English we know.

There were romantic comedies like *The Taming of the Shrew*, in which Petruchio plans to win the heart of hot-tempered Kate by acting like a lunatic. (To "rail" is to complain angrily.)

Say that she rail, why then I'll tell her plain
She sings as sweetly as a nightingale.
Say that she frown, I'll say she looks as clear
As morning roses newly washed with dew. . . .
If she do bid me pack, I'll give her thanks
As though she bid me stay by her a week.

There were tragedies like *King Lear*, in which an aged king gives his kingdom and his power to his two evil daughters and then discovers that they both despise him. He is so furious that he can barely talk:

I will have such revenges on you both
That all the world shall – I will do such things –
What they are, yet I know not; but they shall be
The terrors of the earth. . . .

Historical dramas were often designed to please and flatter Queen Elizabeth. (It was always wise to stay on her good side.) In *Richard II*, Shakespeare tactfully supported Elizabeth's claim to the throne by giving an earlier king a speech that made him sound like a coward, a liar, and a heartless killer:

Is there a murderer here? No. Yes, I am. . . .
O no! Alas, I rather hate myself
For hateful deeds committed by myself.
I am a villain. Yet I lie, I am not. . . .

With Shakespeare and others doing so much writing,

This is thought to be a portrait of Shakespeare (1564-1616), although we can't be sure. He wrote almost forty plays, and probably acted in most of them. He also wrote beautiful poems, especially love sonnets. His work is so brilliant that some people refuse to believe he wrote it; they insist that the writer must have been someone with a nobler family and a better education.

Dr. Thomas Bowdler appreciated Shakespeare's genius, but thought his writing was spoiled by indecent words, scenes, and even plots. In 1807 Bowdler published a new collection of Shakespeare, "improving" the parts he disapproved of. Today, **bowdlerizing** means rewriting someone else's work, changing the parts you find unacceptable.

thousands of new words entered the English language. It's impossible to say how many were actually invented by Shakespeare, but as far as we know, the following (and many others) first appear in his writing: **countless, courtship, critical, excellent, frugal, horrid, leapfrog, lonely**.

He also put together wonderful expressions. He had such a fine ear for the perfect way to say something that we quote him more than any other author – often mindlessly, without hearing the literal meaning of the words. But take a fresh look at these Shakespearean phrases, and see how vividly an image can sum up an idea in just a few words:

barefaced
crack of doom
dead as a doornail
eyesore
flesh and blood
foul play
lily-livered
tongue-tied
tower of strength
vanish into thin air

Most of Shakespeare's plots were not original; he borrowed from real life, ancient myths, and tales from all over Europe. But nobody had told these stories so vividly and powerfully. His works have been translated into innumerable languages. Scholars re-examine them obsessively, writing thousands of books about them, counting how many different words the "Bard of Avon" uses (as many as

What's the difference between these two sentences?

1) Alice will go to the zoo if she can.

2) Alice would go to the zoo if she could.

Doesn't the second sentence tell you that she can't go?

In the past, different "moods" of verbs were used to show whether something was just doubtful (sentence 1), or actually contrary to fact (sentence 2). English has lost many of these distinctions; they were too complicated, and the moods got confused with other forms. But they can still help you make it clear that what you're describing is *not* the way things are. The three examples below describe imaginary situations that are contrary to fact. Can you change them so they mean that you simply *don't know* whether the situation is true or not?

1) If you **had** five dollars he **could** bake you a cake.

2) The warthog **might** still be out there, if the lion **hadn't** chased it away.

3) If I **were** going I **would** have to take a present (but I'm staying home and keeping it for myself!)

ANSWERS

"DOUBTFUL" ANSWERS:

If you **have** five dollars he **can** bake you a cake.

The warthog **may** still be out there, if the lion **hasn't** chased it away.

If I **am** going I **will** have to take a present (but I'd rather stay home and keep it for myself!)

In *Macbeth*, Shakespeare describes three witches as "**weird** sisters." The witches foretell Macbeth's fate (death – though he misunderstands them), and **weird** comes from the Old English *wyrd* meaning fate, "what will be." But over the years, audiences watching these eerie characters have given the word a new meaning: "strange and bizarre."

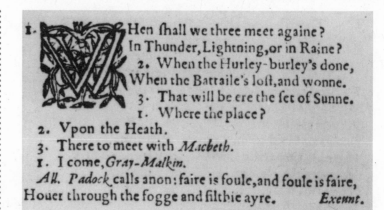

Seven years after Shakespeare died, most of his plays were published in a collection called the First Folio. In this First Folio copy of *Macbeth*, the spelling is not quite like ours. The letters u and v are the same (*V* is the capital), and the long *s* (similar to *f*) replaces our *s* several times in the opening speech by one of the three weird sisters.

thirty thousand, compared to just eight thousand in the King James Bible), even counting his commas (138,198). The plays are presented over and over around the world, sometimes as movies and musicals, sometimes with a twist: Julius Caesar as a businessman in a suit and tie, Romeo and Juliet as New York teenagers separated by warring street gangs.

Yet if Shakespeare had lived before the invention of the printing press, which could turn out hundreds or thousands of scripts, all his plays and poems might easily have been lost forever.

14

GREENER PASTURES

Some of Elizabethan England's new prosperity was coming from South America, through the back door. While Spain had claimed most of that continent, English sea captains were committing outrageous acts of piracy against the Spanish galleons as they lumbered home with their loads of gold and silver and precious gems. Queen Elizabeth pretended to disapprove of the raids, but much of the loot ended up in her treasury. The bold captains were celebrated as heroes, and richly rewarded.

What England really needed, though, was more farmland to feed its growing population. In North America, France was taking over the territory around the St. Lawrence River and the Great Lakes. Spain dominated the areas farther south and west. So the English hoped to start settlements along the east coast, between the two.

In 1607 an English colony was successfully established at Jamestown. In 1620 another group of settlers sailed from

France held much of the northeastern continent, Spain had territories in the south and west, and before long a chain of English fur-trading posts was spreading through the northwest. As European interests expanded, more and more native peoples were driven off their land.

England to Cape Cod, in "New England," on a little ship called the *Mayflower*. Some of them were "Puritans" – people who wanted to "purify" the English religion of its politics and its fancy rituals. In England, Puritans were being persecuted for their beliefs. Those who sailed to America, in hopes of creating a more virtuous "Kingdom of God" where they could live simple, pious lives, are known as the Pilgrims.

The *Mayflower* settlers suffered illness and starvation during the winter of 1620, but with help from the local native people the colony survived. After the harvest of 1621, the colonists and natives joined in a feast of thanksgiving. Their dinner probably wasn't as elegant as this romantic painting suggests, but it did include four wild turkeys, and probably cranberries too – something to think about, next Thanksgiving Day.

We often create a new word by naming something for the place it comes from. Those little raisins called **currants** were once "raisins of Corinth" because they came from around Corinth, in the south of Greece. The island of Cyprus, south of Turkey, gave its name to **copper** (*cyprium* is Latin for "of Cyprus.") **Denim** began as cloth *de Nîmes* – cloth from Nîmes, a town in France.

And then more shiploads of English-speaking settlers arrived, and they started more farms and built more towns. As they spread out across North America and down into the Caribbean, they needed words for all the unfamiliar things around them. Sometimes they stuck together words they already knew: a frog that roared like a bull became a **bullfrog**; a snake that rattled its tail became a **rattlesnake**. Sometimes they borrowed (and mangled) names from native North American languages: *segongw* became **skunk**; *aroughcun* became **raccoon**, *mus* became **moose**, and other native words became **chipmunk**, **pecan**, **squash**, **toboggan**, and so on.

For a few decades in the 1600s, there were Dutch settlements along the east coast, around where New York is today. Some Dutch words were also adapted into English – including **cookie** (*koekje*, little cake), **coleslaw** (*koolsla*, cabbage salad), **waffle**, **sleigh**, and (since this was the time of the great "Dutch Masters" painters) the painting terms **landscape** and **easel**.

In 1763, a treaty ending a war in Europe gave England almost all France's land in North America, and

Another way to create new words is to add onto old ones. A *prefix* turns **think** into **re**think; a *suffix* turns it into **think**ing; with both prefix and suffix we can make **un**think**able**. Most prefixes and suffixes come from Latin or Greek, and they're handy to know. They can help you figure out words you've never seen before. Look at these prefixes, and see if you can answer the questions below.

circum – (around)	**com** – (together)
dys – (bad/difficult)	**poly** – (many)
hypo – (below)	**epi** – (on)

1) If **elocution** is clear speaking, what's **circumlocution**?

2) If a **utopia** is an ideal land, what's a **dystopia**?

3) If a **tripod** is a stand with three feet, what's a **polypod**?

4) If **zoology** is the study of animals, what kind of animal is an **epizoon**?

5) If your **epiglottis** is the little tab that hangs above your tongue, what's a **polyglot**?

6) If **euphoria** is a general sense of feeling good, what is **dysphoria**?

7) If **oxygen** is a gas we need to live, what's **hypoxia**?

8) If your **domicile** is where you live, what's a word for a building where people live together? (This is trickier!)

ANSWERS

1) talking "in circles," not getting to the point

2) a "nightmare" land where you really don't want to live!

3) something with many feet

4) an animal that lives on other animals (like a tick or flea)

5) someone who speaks many languages ("tongues")

6) a general sense of feeling bad (anxious, discontent, etc.)

7) an oxygen level below what the body needs (the extra *o* of hypo-ox*ia* drops out

8) condominium; "com" has become "con" in front of the "d" to be pronounceable. Before an "l" it can become "col," as in collect (bring together). Changes like this often happen over time: *v* becomes *b*, *b* turns into *p*, and so on. If you say the word out loud, it's easier to see the connection.

Spain's Florida territory as well. Some eighty years later, the once-Spanish territories of California and Texas would join English-speaking America. The language of that little island on the other side of the Atlantic – the language that had muddled together the words and rules of so many invaders – was taking over this faraway continent.

Many flowers are named after people who discovered or grew them: Kamel's **camellia**, Dahl's **dahlia**, Magnol's **magnolia**, Poinsett's **poinsettia**. Others take their names from ancient words that suggest their shape. The aster has points like a star (Greek *aster*); part of the **delphinium** suggests a dolphin (Greek *delphin*); a flower with a leaf like a Roman soldier's sword (Latin *gladius*) is a **gladiolus**. As for the **nasturtium**, it can make your nose itch (*nasum torqueat* is Latin for "irritates the nose")!

But what kind of English did the settlers speak? It depended on where they came from, and what level of society. It also depended on when they migrated, for they took with them the speech of that time. From then on, their English and Britain's English would develop in different ways. For example, the Canadian island of Newfoundland is isolated by the long winters and cold, rough waters of the North Atlantic. Fishing folk from Ireland and western England began settling there way back in Shakespeare's day. Because the island was so cut off, their speech developed in its own direction, keeping or inventing words like **brewis** for stew; **slims** for pancakes; **totties** for dandelions. They called a bumblebee a **dumbledore**, your two front teeth were your **butter teeth**, and if you weren't a **livyer** (a real Newfoundlander), you must be from **upalong** – meaning just about anyplace else in Canada or the United States.

> To the Aztecs of Mexico, **coyote** and **ocelot** were *coyotl* and *tlalocelotl*, and **tomato** was *tomatl*. Our word **chocolate** comes from *chocolatl*, but the hot chocolate the Aztecs brewed was dark and bitter, almost coffee-like – no milk, no sugar, no marshmallows!

From Africa we get **banana, chimpanzee, tote,** and **voodoo**. From the Spanish of the American West we get **bonanza, ranch, rodeo, plaza, stampede, canyon, bronco,** and **tornado**. English also borrowed words the Spanish had adopted from native people farther south: **barbecue, canoe,** and **potato** from Haiti; **condor** and **puma** from Peru; **hammock, hurricane, manatee,** and **tobacco** from the Caribs, who gave their name to the Caribbean Sea.

The way people spoke also depended on where they moved to. Perhaps there was already a local population with a certain way of speaking. Perhaps there was a strong Spanish or French influence. Perhaps there were Africans who had been shipped in to labor as slaves in the fields and homes. All these would influence the speech of new arrivals, and their children and grandchildren. In the Caribbean particularly, the jumble of languages – from native people, early explorers, sailors, Africans, and settlers – grew (and is still growing) into versions of English that sound almost like whole new languages.

What about their writing? The first colonial writers were driven by their religion, and their determination to found a better and fairer society. They wrote sermons and prayers and lectures, not thrilling dramas and romances that might waste people's time and lead them into temptation. Cotton Mather, a solemn scholar and historian, was a Puritan minister around 1700, and a grandson of two Puritan ministers who had fled England to find religious freedom. This is from his "Christian" account of how the colonists triumphed over the native people (or "Salvages," as he calls them):

> The Flame of War then Raged thro' a great
> part of the Country, whereby many whole
> Towns were Laid in Ashes, and many Lives
> were Sacrificed. But in little more than one
> years Time, the United Colonies . . . bravely
> Conquered the Salvages. The Evident Hand of
> Heaven appearing on the Side of a people
> whose Hope and Help was alone in the
> Almighty Lord of Hosts, Extinguished whole
> Nations of the Salvages at such a rate, that
> there can hardly any of them now be found . . .
> upon the face of the Earth.

Just after Mather died in 1728, a young American named Benjamin Franklin began an extraordinary career as a writer and editor – and scientist and inventor and statesman and many other things as well. Franklin disliked pompous language – "Here comes the Orator!" he wrote, "with his Flood of Words, and his Drop of Reason." His writing combined Puritan values like honesty and hard work with humor, common sense, and immense intelligence and learning. When he was twenty, he resolved to set out a plan for his life:

I am now entering upon a new [life]: let me, therefore, make some resolutions, and form some scheme of action, that, henceforth, I may live in all respects like a rational creature.

His resolutions included being "extremely frugal" till his debts were paid, being truthful and sincere "in every word and action," being industrious in his work, and never speaking ill of anyone, "not even in a matter of truth."

Ben Franklin (1706-90) dropped out of school at age ten to help his father make soap and candles, became an apprentice in journalism, and then published his own magazines – including *"Poor Richard's" Almanack*, written under the pen name of Richard Saunders. Franklin started a circulating library, a debating club, a hospital, and an academy that grew into a university. He studied science, especially the mystery of electricity, and proved that lightning was electric. He traveled widely, learned foreign languages, worked in various levels of government, reorganized the post office, invented bifocal glasses and the Franklin woodstove, and was a key contributor to the American Declaration of Independence and the Constitution of the United States.

While more and more settlers headed west from Britain, hoping for a better life in the New World, ships were sailing in the opposite direction for a very different reason. They carried not pilgrims but prisoners, men and women convicted of various crimes. Britain's prisons were desperately overcrowded and full of disease, and the government wanted to transport some of the inmates to a far-off land where they would make no more trouble. In 1787, eleven convict ships set out for Australia. Over the next eighty years, many more would follow.

Those convicts who were lucky enough to survive the years of their sentence sometimes remained in Australia, and law-abiding settlers began moving there as well, to raise sheep for wool, or to start other businesses. Since they were even more isolated than Newfoundlanders, they developed their own words and ways of saying them; once again, the English language was shifting shape. Some words were adopted from the native Aboriginal people, such as **boomerang** and many plant and animal names: **kiwi**, **kangaroo**, **wombat**, **kookaburra**. Others were adapted or invented: **outback** (the barren interior), **bushman** (an expert traveler in the outback). With jokey suffixes, barbecue and tin can and Christmas became **barbie** and **tinnie** and **Chrissy**.

In some colonial areas, native people invented their own twist on English, known as "pidgin." (The name is a mangling of "business," since it lets people work together even if they all speak different languages.) Pidgin languages use a minimum number of words – some English, some not – and very basic grammar. In Tok Pisin – the pidgin talk of Papua New Guinea, north of Australia – anything large is *bigpela* ("big fellow"); possession is shown by *bilong* ("belongs to"); *meri* (from "Virgin Mary") means "woman," *na* means "and." So *gras bilong fes* is a beard (face-grass), and a *bigpela haus buk bilong ol man na meri* is a big house of books for all men and women – a public library. Pidgin may seem roundabout, but it covers a host of meanings as simply as possible. It's a language of its own.

**Can you guess what these Tok Pisin phrases mean?
Listen to the sounds of the words. Here are two hints:
kaikai means "food" and *pikinini* means "child."**

1) Mi laikim kaikai bilong moningtaim.

2) Man nogut i stilim kar.

3) Hamas yias bilong yu?

4) Nek bilong mi i drai.

5) Mi lukim nambawan pikinini bilong Misis Kwin.

ANSWERS

1) I'd like breakfast (food that belongs in the morningtime).

2) A bad (no-good) man stole the car.

3) How old (how much years) are you?

4) I'm thirsty (my neck is dry).

5) I saw Prince Charles (the queen's number-one child).

15

THE WAR BETWEEN ENGLISH & ENGLISH

As England's colonies south of the Great Lakes grew larger and richer and stronger, many people there resented being ruled (and taxed!) by a small country far across the Atlantic. In the 1770s these colonies went to war, breaking away from Britain and creating an independent America. Thousands of Loyalists – people who preferred to remain British – moved north into Canada, which still belonged to Britain.

Even after winning their independence, many Americans still resented all things English. A few thought Americans should all speak French – or even Greek – to teach England a lesson. But most people realized that it would be ridiculous to give up the language altogether. Instead, they would start speaking and writing English in their own way. They would make it simpler. More sensible. And better, of course.

One of these anti-English Americans, Noah Webster,

Noah Webster (1758-1843) was a schoolteacher, and also a magazine publisher, a lawyer, a lecturer, and an outspoken opponent of slavery.

saw the new country as a utopia of liberty and virtue. In 1789 – not long after the American states became independent – he predicted that their English would become a different language altogether. It would even use a different alphabet, with added letters and accents, to spell every word the way it sounded. **Health**, **neighbor**, and **tongue** would become **helth**, **nabor**, and **tung**. "There iz no alternativ," he declared. "A *national language* is a brand of *national union*." In the name of independence and patriotism, Americans should speak American.

How good is your *English* English? Can you translate these British words into North American?

1) Hold the baby for a moment, I'll get a **nappy** from the **boot**.

2) The way that **lorry** is parked, it's blocking the **dustmen**.

3) I didn't go and get the **post** because the **lift** was broken.

4) There's a **coach** up there on the **flyover**.

5) Do you want an **ice lolly** for **afters**?

6) I'm going to the **chemist's**. Play **noughts and crosses** till I get back.

ANSWERS

1) Hold the baby for a moment, I'll get a diaper from the car trunk.

2) The way that truck is parked, it's blocking the garbage collectors.

3) I didn't go and get the mail because the elevator was broken.

4) There's a bus up there on the overpass.

5) Do you want an ice cream treat for dessert?

6) I'm going to the drugstore. Play Xs and Os till I get back.

Just a few decades earlier, some people back in England had also been dissatisfied with their language. They complained that English was not properly defined, the way Latin and Greek were. Words were used in too many different ways. Grammar and spelling were inconsistent. Meanings kept changing, and sloppy expressions were slipping in. It was time for some expert to write a rule book everyone could follow, so that English would be preserved for ever. After all, if the language kept changing, future generations wouldn't be able to read the treasures of English literature. In 1722, Jonathan Swift — who was in the midst of writing *Gulliver's Travels* – published an impassioned letter addressed to Britain's Lord High Treasurer, asking him how any author could be expected to go on working

> with Spirit and Chearfulness, when he considers, that he will be read with Pleasure but a very few Years, and in an Age or two shall hardly be understood without an Interpreter? This is like employing an excellent Statuary [sculptor] to work upon mouldring Stone.

Defining a language that had grown out of so many sources, over so many centuries, was a huge challenge. But one man stepped up to it – a brilliant writer and scholar named Samuel Johnson. It was time, he said, to rid English of its impurities – its "barbarous corruptions, licentious idioms and colloquial barbarisms." He and a few assistants spent nine years writing an authoritative English dictionary. Johnson came up with definitions for over forty-three thou-

Samuel Johnson (1708-1784) had problems with his vision and hearing, and suffered ill health for most of his life. He was generally gloomy and depressed, and often irritable, even rude. His father owned a bookshop, and Johnson grew up reading English, Latin, and Greek. He went to Oxford University for a while but couldn't afford to stay, so he dropped out to work as a bookseller, teacher, and journalist. But after his dictionary was published, the government gave him a pension, Oxford University gave him a doctorate, and he became known as "Dictionary Johnson," the foremost expert on the English language.

In the 1700s there was a kind of writing paper that had a watermark (faint pattern) like a fool (a court jester) or a fool's cap. Three hundred years later, we still call legal-sized paper **foolscap**.

sand words, indicating how each word was said, the part of speech, and the derivation. By including one hundred and eighteen thousand quotations from well-known authors, he showed various ways the words could be used, and how their meanings had changed over the centuries. For good measure, he threw in a history of the English language, and a guide to grammar.

The result, published in 1755, was the first great English dictionary. For a hundred years it was the standard reference book that families trusted and relied on. It also gave future lexicographers (dictionary writers) a foundation to build on, to create their own dictionaries. Even today, many of

Johnson's definitions appear in modern dictionaries.

There had been dictionaries before then, but most had been guidebooks to rare or difficult words. Johnson was the first lexicographer to include all kinds of day-to-day words. (He defined **lexicographer** as "A writer of dictionaries, a harmless drudge. . . .") He also made some general decisions. For example, what was the right spelling of words like **color/colour** and **center/centre**? Some people argued that words from French should have French endings and words from Latin should have Latin endings. But since English came from both Latin and French, and since French itself came from Latin, who could say which words began where? Resolving to settle the matter, Johnson decided on the *our* (**colour**) and *re* (**centre**) endings.

As for Noah Webster, over in America, by 1800 he had published several schoolbooks, including a wildly popular spelling book that eventually sold some *400 million* copies. He began working on his own dictionary, using Johnson's book as a base and noting his additions and changes in the margins. He included some specifically American words, and defined an American style of spelling and pronunciation. For twenty-five years Webster labored alone, compiling entries for seventy thousand words and writing them all by hand. His dictionary, published in 1828, cut many double consonants down to singles, and used the *or* and *er* endings that Johnson had rejected. That's why Americans today have **jewelers** with **honor**, the British have **jewellers** with **honour**, and other English-speaking countries have to pick one side or the other.

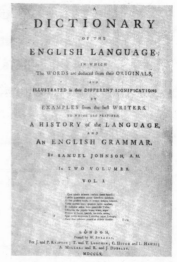

The title page of Johnson's dictionary, published in 1755, "in which the WORDS are deduced from their ORIGINALS, and ILLUSTRATED in their DIFFERENT SIGNIFICATIONS by EXAMPLES from the best WRITERS." But a greater dictionary was yet to come. In 1928, after seventy years of work by numerous editors and thousands of volunteers, *The Oxford English Dictionary* was completed. It filled twelve immense volumes — "fat, heavy, shelf-bendingly huge" — with more than four hundred thousand words, and almost two million quotations. One of the many assistants who worked on it was Tolkien, author of *Lord of the Rings*; he was assigned to the letter *w*, and wrestled with words like **wallop**, **walrus**, and **wasp**.

We take dictionaries for granted these days, but stop and think for a moment. Isn't it difficult to think of a brief, clear explanation of even a basic word? How would you define *to walk*? And *to laugh*?

JOHNSON'S DICTIONARY DEFINITIONS:

TO WALK: 1. To move by leisurely steps, so that one foot is set down, before the other is taken up. . . .

TO LAUGH: 1. To make that noise which sudden merriment excites.

Dictionaries are handy for telling us what words mean, and how to spell and pronounce them. But why do we need them for short, simple words – like **run**, from Old English *rinnan*, "to set in motion"? The word is easy to say and easy to explain, isn't it? Running is like walking, only faster.

But running is also what a motor does when it's working. It's what water does when it's flowing. It's what color does when it leaks out of fabric. You can run a movie or run a business or run a crook out of town. **Run** can be a noun: there are baseball runs and toboggan runs, stocking runs and runs on the stock market. And then there's the present participle, **running**. (Participles are verbs used like adjectives, to describe nouns.) There are running boards, running lights, running mates, and running stitches. If you check a dictionary, you'll see that **run** is used in a lot of other ways as well. And that's just one small word!

Have you ever meant one word, and said another in-

See if you can fill in some other runs.

Try a prefix in front:

1) A movie you've already seen is a _____.

2) Somebody faster can _____ you.

Try a suffix after:

3) Butter left in the sun gets _____.

4) A small motorboat is a _____.

5) Someone who won't give you a straight answer is giving you the _____.

Now try adding an adverb or a preposition:

6) If you're slow, time can run _____.

7) Pour too fast, and your cup will run _____.

8) A car can run _____ a lamp post.

9) To practice a piano piece, you run _____ it many times.

10) A flag is run _____ the flagpole.

11) An unwound clock will run _____.

12) The cost of something can run _____ twenty dollars.

13) Throw a ball, and your dog will run _____ it. (Maybe.)

Spoonerisms are another mistake people fall into when they speak carelessly. Reverend Spooner, a dean at Oxford University around 1890, was famous for mixing up the beginnings of his words, saying "a scoop of Boy Trouts" meaning "a troop of Boy Scouts," or "a well-boiled icicle" for "a well-oiled bicycle." It's not clear how many spoonerisms really came from the reverend – mischievous students may have invented some of them – but Spooner buries the claim – sorry, carries the blame. Pea soup? Be careful how you say it!

stead? This can happen in a moment of brain-scramble, when we're tired or not paying attention. Other times, we use a word we have heard, maybe to sound clever, and – oops! – it doesn't mean what we thought it did.

Over two hundred years ago, the Irish playwright Richard Brinsley Sheridan invented a character called Mrs. Malaprop who does exactly this. (Her name comes from French *mal à propos*, "out of place.") Straining to speak elegantly, Mrs. Malaprop says "illegible" when she means "ineligible," confuses a "pineapple" with a "pinnacle," and imagines a scaly "allegory" sunning itself on the banks of the Nile.

Imagine a malapropist trying to impress a high muck-a-muck: "Oh please, your exultation, not a syllabub of apoplexy. I would never ask someone of your extinction to defenestrate himself for a person as incontinent as myself."

1) What does this garbler mean to say?
2) What is really coming out?

ANSWERS

1) "Oh please, your excellency, not a syllable of apology. I would never ask someone of your distinction to be deferential to a person as inconsequential as myself."

2) "Oh please, your joyfulness, not a pudding of stroke. I would never ask someone of your destruction to throw himself out a window for a person as uncontrollable as myself."

Do you remember Alice, who visited Wonderland and then met Humpty Dumpty in the land behind the looking-glass (mirror)?

> "When *I* use a word," Humpty Dumpty said in rather a scornful tone, "it means just what I choose it to mean – neither more nor less."
>
> "The question is," said Alice, "whether you *can* make words mean so many different things."

The more a word is misused, the more mixed up people get about what it's supposed to mean. Eventually both meanings, old and new, end up in dictionaries, because most dictionaries report what people are actually saying, even when the meaning has become muddled. And pretty soon, when you hear or read the word, you can't be sure which meaning is intended. English grows and changes over time, of course. But careless, sloppy mistakes damage the language, instead of making it richer and stronger.

Here are a few examples of words being mixed up these days:

imply (suggest) and **infer** (deduce)
"No, I'm not implying that you stole my watch. But from the watch strap hanging out of your pocket, I infer that you stole somebody's."

flout (refuse to obey) and **flaunt** (show off)
Brittany flouted the dress code to flaunt her new miniskirt.

fortuitous (by chance) and **fortunate** (lucky)
Our fortuitous meeting with the karate teacher turned out to be fortunate; a few minutes later, a bully demanded our lunch money.

literally (actually) and **figuratively** (so to speak)
My dad says he's literally drooling for dinner. That makes him sound like the dog! I hope he means "figuratively."

problem and **dilemma** (a choice between two options when you don't like either one)
If I tell my dad I lost my math problems, he won't let me go to the movies – but if I tell my mom, she'll make me clean my room. What a dilemma!

disinterested (unbiased) and **uninterested** (not interested)
We offered Ajay a dollar to act as a disinterested umpire, but he had just got his allowance so he was uninterested.

mano a mano (by fighting; Spanish for "hand to hand") and **man to man**
Phil and Franco were threatening to settle their argument mano a mano, but eventually they talked it out man to man.

Even the stress on a word – the syllable we say more loudly – can be confusing. How do you say **produce, rebel, record, research**, and **address**? This is a trick question, because all these words can be either a noun or a verb. In Shakespeare's day they were all stressed on the second syllable – proDUCE, reBEL – but since then, the stress on the nouns has tended to shift forward to the first syllable. A farmer proDUCEs PROduce. A REbel reBELS. You addRESS an envelope with an ADDress, preSENT a PREsent, and reCORD a REcord.

Or maybe you don't – because these words are still changing, and how you say them depends on who you are and where you live. Will other words shift their stress in the same way? Will we someday misTAKE our MIStake and rePEAT a REpeat? Who knows?

With so many words to learn, how can you keep them straight? Think of Samuel Johnson and Noah Webster, and reach for a dictionary. It's not just for spelling. It's a user's guide to the English language.

16 BRITANNIA'S HEYDAY

Before the 1800s, trips to distant lands were slow, uncomfortable, and often dangerous. The wealthy might travel for amusement, taking heaps of luggage and an army of servants. Some adventurers headed off alone, daring the risks and hardships and hoping for the best. But most people only left home if they had to; otherwise, they lived out their lives in the neighborhoods where they had been born.

In any case, Europe was a dangerous place for a holiday. After the French Revolution in 1789, and the beheading of the king and queen, Napoleon had taken control of France, and had crowned himself emperor. His armies were on the march as he extended his empire west into Spain, south into Italy, and east across Europe and into Russia.

But Napoleon was defeated in 1815, and much of his empire collapsed, while the British empire was flourishing. The British flag flew over territories not just in the

Americas and Australia, but also in the Mediterranean, the East Indies, the Far East, Africa, and countless islands scattered around the globe. The British boasted that the sun never set on their empire; "Our tongue is known in every clime, our flag on every sea."

By this time, travel was not only safer; it was easier than ever before. Thanks to the inventions of the Industrial Revolution, railways whisked passengers over iron bridges spanning deep valleys, and through tunnels blasted under mountains. Ships chugged along on steam power, no longer waiting for wind to fill their sails. By the 1850s you could even buy a package tour, with the tedious details of tickets and hotels and meals arranged in advance.

Tourists were drawn to Italy by ancient Roman ruins and by spectacular buildings like St. Mark's Basilica, in Venice — so grand, so elaborate, so excitingly foreign.

Tourism – especially the "grand tour" of major cities and antiquities – became the rage. Travelers returned home entranced by foreign styles of art, architecture, landscaping, cooking, clothing, music, and dance. Wherever the English went, their language went too – and brought home new words in its baggage.

In 1869 the Suez Canal opened, linking the Mediterranean and the Red Sea so that ships could head east without making the long, dangerous trip around the bottom of Africa. The voyage to India, once an ordeal of many months, could be done through the canal in just seventeen days. This was vital for the British, because by now much of India was part of their empire.

India was a thrilling destination, with its elephants and tigers, its snake charmers, its elaborate temples and romantic palaces. In the evening, travelers could return to a British-style hotel, order roast beef and Yorkshire pudding, and settle down to read a London newspaper, though it might be a few weeks old.

Back in 1600, in the days of Elizabeth I, a group of merchants had formed the East India Company, to send out great sailing ships (called East Indiamen) that would bring back exotic goods like pepper and other spices, and gems, and indigo (blue) dye. By 1700 the East India Company owned territories around India, and was shipping tea and coffee and printed fabrics. By 1800 the company had its own army and navy. British soldiers, government officials, teachers, missionaries, and merchants lived there, many with their families. Indian servants cleaned their houses, cooked their dinners, and cared for their children. Inevitably, words from Hindi and other Indian languages crept into English.

Our word **guru** (teacher, expert) is a Hindi word, and **pundit** (also meaning expert) comes from *pandit*, Hindi for scholar; Jawaharlal Nehru, one of India's prime ministers, was known as Pandit Nehru. **Bungalow** began as *bangla*, "Bengal-style" – light one-story houses must have been common in the steamy Bengal region of India. **Chintz** (flowered cotton fabric) was called *chints* in Hindi. The small rowboat we call a **dinghy** started out as a *dingi*, **jungle** comes from *jangal*, **thug** from *thag*. **Veranda** began as *varanda*, **bangle** as *bangri*, **loot** as *lut*, and **shampoo** as *chhampo*. The British in India developed a taste for hot **curry** (*kari* in Tamil) and **chutney** (*chatni*). Even the British nickname for their homeland – **Old Blighty** – came from Hindi; *bilayati* meant "foreign."

Have you ever heard of a **juggernaut**? It's something immense and almost unstoppable — like an eighteen-wheeler barreling down the highway. In the Hindu religion, Jagannath is an avatar (form) of the great god Vishnu. (His name comes from Sanskrit *jagat nathas*, "world protector.") Jagannath's statue is paraded through the streets of India in a heavy cart. It's said that some fervent worshippers used to hurl themselves under the cart's giant wheels.

Since the English weren't the only ones bringing home new vocabulary, some words ended up with a tangled history. For example, workers in Iraq, in a part of Baghdad called *attabiy*, used to make glossy striped silk. Italians called the cloth *tabi*. The English turned *tabi* into **tabby** – and pretty soon, glossy striped cats were called **tabbies**.

By the early 1800s, English tourists were flocking to the cities and health spas of Europe's German-speaking states – Prussia, Bavaria, Austria, and many others. After all, the English and the Germans were almost cousins. Queen Victoria, who reigned from 1837 till 1901, was partly German; her husband was German; their oldest daughter married the crown prince of Germany. German literature was greatly admired, while German music – Beethoven, Schubert, Schumann, Wagner – was unparalleled. How could one be cultured without speaking at least a smattering of German?

German looks daunting at first, partly because the words can be stuck together like beads on a string. This creates phrase-words that are useful for combining ideas that really don't fit in one word – like *Kindergarten*, "child-garden." (Unlike English nouns, German nouns still begin with capital letters.) Here are some other German constructions that have slipped into English:

Bildungsroman (education-novel): a novel about someone growing up. The Harry Potter books add up to a **bildungsroman**.

Schadenfreude (harm-joy): pleasure from someone else's misfortune; "After Terry stole my toffee, I felt a thrill of **schadenfreude** when he pulled out one of his fillings."

Doppelganger (double-goer): a stranger who looks exactly like someone else. When a **doppelganger** appears in a story, it usually means something spooky is going to happen!

With many words run together like this, German offers less choice about the order that words are put in. Often an important word like the main verb comes right at the end of the sentence:

Der Unfall war in zwei Sekunden geschehen.
The accident had in two seconds happened.

In English we have a lot of freedom about how we arrange our words. We can choose a certain order because it makes the sense clearer, or it sounds better, or it's less boring. But it's generally wise to keep modifiers close to whatever they describe. Look what can happen when you don't:

I'm going to say I'm leaving tomorrow. (Are you *leaving* tomorrow? Or are you *saying* tomorrow that you'll leave some other time?) The adverb, **tomorrow,** should be close to the verb it modifies – but is that **leaving?** Or **going to say?**

I took my puppy to the vet, who has droopy ears and a waggly tail. Oops! The modifying clause, "who has droopy ears and a waggly tail," should be close to **puppy.**

While some English words come from the depths of history and some are from foreign languages, others were deliberately invented. Lewis Carroll, the creator of *Alice in Wonderland* and *Alice through the Looking-Glass*, invented many words, including **slithy** and **mimsy**. Meaning what? "Well," Humpty Dumpty explains to Alice, "'slithy' means 'lithe and slimy'. . . You see it's like a portmanteau – there

What's a dangling participle? Remember that a participle is a form of verb that, like an adjective, modifies a noun – "the **escaped** rhinoceros," "the **fleeing** crowd." If the participle is too far from what it modifies, we say it's dangling; it's not attached to the correct word, so it gloms onto whatever is nearby:

After **chomping** on the dragonfly, <u>we</u> saw the frog swallow. (Yuck! The participle, **chomping**, should be close to **frog**.)

Dressed in her tutu, <u>the cat</u> and the ballerina looked lovely. (Miaow!)

Sometimes, whatever the participle was supposed to describe isn't even in the sentence:

Getting up next morning, <u>the house</u> was cold.

Driving into the forest, <u>the mountain</u> disappeared. (How far up did the house get? Does that mountain have a driver's license?)

are two meanings packed up into one word." (**Portman-teau** is an old name for a suitcase, from the French for "carry-coat.") "Well then," he goes on, "'mimsy' is 'flimsy and miserable' (there's another portmanteau for you.)"

 Galumph blends **gallop** and **triumphant** ("My dog finally found her ball, and came **galumphing** back to me." A guesstimate is an estimate based on guesswork, and **smash** is part **smack** and part **mash**.

Do you know these portmanteau words? If not, can you figure them out?

1) What's the name of the tunnel under the English Channel?

2) What's a bit like breakfast and a bit like lunch?

3) What's halfway between a snort and a chuckle?

4) What kind of dog is part Labrador and part poodle?

5) What's a cross between broccoli and cauliflower?

6) What's partly a skirt and partly shorts?

7) How do we describe a day that's gray and drizzly?

8) What are we breathing when fog mixes with smoky pollution?

ANSWERS

PORTMANTEAU WORDS	
1) the Channel	5) broccoflower
2) brunch	6) skort
3) chortle	7) grizzly
4) Labradoodle	8) smog

Sometimes we create a language so that people *won't* understand us. Kids try to fool their parents by speaking pig Latin – not Latin at all, but English mangled so that "hide the book" becomes "ide-hay e-thay ook-bay" (though their parents probably spoke pig Latin when they were young). Each generation invents its own slang, its own private vocabulary, especially for common meanings like **excellent** or **disgusting** or **boring**. Can you think of special words that you and your friends use? Words you don't expect to hear from your parents or grandparents? They probably had their own slang words, when they were your age.

Although most biscuits are baked only once, **biscuit** is derived from Latin *biscoctu*, "twice-cooked." Those long, thin Italian cookies called **biscotti** are baked twice – first in a loaf, and then again in slices. So is **zwieback**, a crisp bread baked till it's brittle all the way through – the name comes from German *zwei backen*, "twice baked."

Can you guess the meanings of these slang expressions from not so very long ago?

1) groanbox
2) have a cow
3) pucker paint
4) make like a boid (bird)
5) the bee's knees
6) the cat's pajamas

ANSWERS

SLANG WORDS

1) accordion
2) get upset
3) lipstick
4) go away
5, 6) the absolute BEST

We know now that the tropical disease called **malaria** is spread by mosquitoes. In the past, though, people thought you caught malaria by breathing infected air – "bad air" – in Italian, *mal'aria*.

French street slang reverses a word's syllables, or at least its sounds. *Café* becomes *féca*, *bonjour* becomes *jour-bon*, *fou* ("crazy") becomes *ouf*. *L'envers*, meaning "reverse," becomes *vers-l'en* (the *s* is silent), or *verlan*, the name of this slang.

Trickiest of all is the rhyming slang of the Cockneys (people from a region of London). It works like this: take the word you mean (such as **phone**) and replace it with an expression that rhymes (**dog and bone**) – "Quiet, I'm on the dog and bone." And if you want to be really mystifying, *drop the part that rhymes*. Then **phone** becomes **dog** – "Quiet, I'm on the dog" – but unless you already know that, good luck figuring it out!

For Britons making the grand tour, Italy was also a must-see destination. Besides, the language was far easier to learn than German. Because Italian is closely related to Latin, many words resemble their English relatives.

The years of easy travel were not to last. The German states, already joined in a confederation to protect their mutual interests, were drawing closer together. By 1871, after a war with Prussia and a war with France, Germany declared itself an empire. The daughter of Queen Victoria was now, awkwardly, the Empress of Germany. Europe was seething with rivalry and resentment.

In 1914, the age of world wars began.

See if you can match these definitions
to words borrowed from Italian:

1) a lively, vivacious way of playing music

2) a course of food served before pasta (noodles)

3) speaking in a soft and subtle voice

4) a porch with a roof supported by columns

5) a woman who sings divinely, like a goddess

6) painting with bright, clear areas and dark, obscured areas

7) coffee brewed by high-pressure steam

8) a painting done on fresh plaster

a) *espresso*

b) *diva*

c) *fresco*

d) *sotto voce*

e) *antipasto*

f) *vivace*

g) *chiaroscuro*

h) *portico*

ANSWERS

4-h	8-c
3-d	7-a
2-e	6-g
1-f	5-b

17

WORDS, WORDS, WORDS

The ancient Greeks and Romans invented countless ways of hurling things at their enemies, including the ballista (from Greek *ballein*, "to throw") – a heavy wooden contraption, similar to a crossbow, that fired a rock or spear. Since a **missile** (from Latin *missum*, "sent") is anything thrown or shot, many early "ballistic missiles" were just big rocks.

War has been a frequent visitor in our history, and it too has added to the English language. The Romans had hundreds of military words – for ranks, weapons, armor, strategies – and some of them remained in Britain after Rome's armies went home. A *cohors* was a unit of several hundred soldiers, a *legio* was ten *cohortes, militia* was military service. To us, **cohorts** are people working together; **legion** means "many"; a **militia** is a group of civilians who are trained to fight in time of war.

When William the Conqueror ferried his Norman horsemen (*chevaliers*, from French *cheval*, "horse") across the English Channel, he brought along the language of cavalry. A **cavalcade** used to be a horse parade, but now it's a special series like "a cavalcade of films." A **cavalier** was once a gallant gentleman like a knight, but today being cavalier means being rather arrogant and inconsiderate: "I said Max could taste my birthday cake, but he's pretty cavalier to take three slices."

Ancient sea battles depended on primitive tactics like ramming or hurling stones, trying to punch holes in the enemy's boats. But sometime in the 1300s, Europeans learned about the explosive force of gunpowder (probably from the Arabs, though it was first invented in China). When the fleet of the Spanish Armada set sail in 1588, it was bristling with **cannons** (from Latin *canna*, "tube"), and the goal was to blast England's ships to smithereens. With gunpowder came words like **detonate**, "explode loudly" (related to Latin *tonare*, "thunder"), and **bomb** and **bombard** (from Greek *bombos*, "booming"). Originally, a bombard was a kind of cannon. Today it's a persistent attack, but not necessarily with guns – "That new kid bombarded me with questions."

By the time of the twentieth century and the two world wars, combat had spread up into the skies, and down into the ocean. Once again, new words were needed. Some came from German: **snorkel** from *Schnorchel*, the tube that lets a submarine breathe without surfacing; **blitz** from *Blitzkrieg*, "lightning war." Today a blitz can be as trivial as an advertising campaign or a football play; in World War II it meant a campaign of sudden, deadly attacks.

Other military words came from Greek: **helicopter** from *helikos pteron*, "whirling wing," and **periscope** – a tube that lets a submarine crew see without surfacing – from *peri skopein*, "around-look."

Some complex inventions just couldn't be defined in one word. Instead of sticking words together, as the Germans

Bomb and **bombard** are "imitative" words; they sound like what they mean. Many imitative words begin with a **sibilant** sound like *s*: **screech**, **spit**, **splash**, **squawk**, **squeal**. (*Sibilus* is Latin for "hissing.") There are heavy words (**bump**, **clump**, **thump**), swingy words (**swirl**, **sway**, **sweep**), glowing words (**gleam**, **glare**, **glitter**). We can **whoop** or **whistle**; we can **whack**, **wham**, or **whomp**. Other words imitate natural reactions: **eek**, **ugh**, **blah**, **pooey**, **yum**, *OW!*

did, anglophones turned to acronyms, made from the beginnings of words. **Radar** detects objects like planes or ships, and determines their distance (range), by bouncing radio waves off them; the name comes from "<u>ra</u>dio <u>d</u>etecting <u>a</u>nd <u>r</u>anging." **Sonar** locates underwater objects by using sound waves: "<u>so</u>und <u>n</u>avigation <u>a</u>nd <u>r</u>anging." We say **flak** meaning angry complaints ("Tanesha got a lot of flak for bringing her pet porcupine to school.") but it began as a wartime acronym from the German for "anti-aircraft gun," *Fliegerabwehrkanone* (flight-defence-cannon).

Acronyms are pronounced as words (NATO, UNICEF), unlike **initialisms**, which are spelled out (FBI, DVD). ("Acronym" comes from Greek *akros onoma*, "at the top [of the] name.") Acronyms and initialisms are both handy shortcuts, but it's easy to forget what they stand for. Do you know the words behind these?

1) OPEC	3) navy SEAL	5) scuba	7) a.m.
2) AWOL	4) op-ed page	6) RSVP	8) RIP

ANSWERS

ACRONYMS AND INITIALISMS

1) <u>O</u>rganization of <u>P</u>etroleum <u>E</u>xporting <u>C</u>ountries

2) <u>a</u>bsent <u>w</u>ithout <u>l</u>eave (the military term for "playing hooky")

3) commando trained to operate on <u>Se</u>a, <u>Ai</u>r, or <u>L</u>and

4) <u>op</u>posite <u>ed</u>itorial – newspaper page facing the editorial page, often featuring letters from readers

5) <u>s</u>elf-<u>c</u>ontained <u>u</u>nderwater <u>b</u>reathing <u>a</u>pparatus

6) *répondez s'il vous plaît* (on an invitation); French for "please respond," meaning "tell us whether you plan to come."

7) *ante meridiem*, Latin for "before noon"

8) *requiescat in pace* (on a tomb, for example) – Latin for "rest in peace," which conveniently has the same initials

In the 1900s, anti-Semitism drove many Jewish people out of Europe, to England and other anglophone lands. Most spoke Yiddish as their everyday language, and Yiddish words spread into English. Yiddish – the name comes from German *judisch*, "Jewish" – is similar to German but it's written in Hebrew characters. (Hebrew, Israel's official language, is used for religion and scholarship.)

Many people think **SOS** – the Morse code message sent by telegraph when a ship is in desperate trouble – means "<u>s</u>ave <u>o</u>ur <u>s</u>ouls." In fact, it was chosen because in Morse code, S-O-S – *di-di-dit, dah-dah-dah, di-di-dit* – is easy to remember and recognize. When ships communicate in English, the emergency message is **mayday, mayday**, from French *m'aidez, m'aidez*, meaning "help me, help me."

Do you know the meanings of these words from Yiddish? (*Ch* is pronounced *h*, and *sch* is pronounced *sh*.)

1) chutzpah
2) kibitz
3) schnozz

4) schmooze
5) shlep
6) schmaltz

ANSWERS

WORDS FROM YIDDISH

1) nerve; "How dare he say that! What chutzpah!"

2) fool around, be a nuisance; "We stopped playing Scrabble because my brother wouldn't stop kibitzing."

3) nose; "You've got marshmallow on your schnozz!"

4) gossip, chat; "Jean's too busy schmoozing to work."

5) drag, haul; "Shlep your homework over here and we'll study together."

6) cooking fat, but often used to mean drippy sentiment; "I got two funny valentines and one schmaltzy one."

A nanosecond –
a billionth of a second –
takes its name from
Greek *nanos,* "dwarf."
A **googol** is the number
you get when you put a
hundred zeroes after "1,"
and it was apparently
named by the nine-year-
old nephew of a mathe-
matician. He defined an
even bigger number, a
googolplex, as "one,
followed by writing
zeroes until you get
tired" – so many zeroes
that if you turned the
whole universe into
paper and ink, you
still couldn't write
them all down.

By the 1950s and the Cold War – the armed standoff between the Communist dictatorships of the east and the democracies of the west – the race for power reached out into space, as both sides built rockets and satellites. Along with the space race came computer technology, with words for things that are unimaginably tiny and fast. Science in general was booming, coming up with new products, new processes, new ideas – and words and more words. Back in the early 1900s, about a thousand new words entered English every year. By the end of that century, the number added each year was close to *twenty thousand.*

Because scientists cooperate internationally, it makes sense to derive new words from Greek and Latin, so they're familiar in many languages. Besides, classical words often sound so grand: **stratosphere** and **troposphere**, **intermolecular** and **intergalactic**, **supersonic** and **supernova**. Need a name for a scientist who studies fossils of prehistoric spiders? Reach for the Greek: *palaios* ("ancient"), *arakhne* ("spider"), and *logos* ("word, talk, discussion") add up to **paleoarachnologist**.

Still, many of our technical terms are old-fashioned English words with new meanings. Look at computer vocabulary: we **boot** up, use a **mouse** and a **menu**, put up a **firewall** so nobody can **hack** into the system, track down a **bug**, **surf** the **net**, set a **bookmark**, and delete any **cookies**. We call one of the great mysteries of space a **black hole**, and dream of finding a shortcut across the universe through a **wormhole** – using words that date back to King Alfred and beyond: *wyrm, blaec, hol.*

Big words, small words, new words, old words,

Anglo-Saxon words, imported words – the richness of the English language gives us so many ways to say pretty much the same thing. How do you go about speaking and writing well? Here's a good place to start: *Think about exactly what you mean, and then say it, simply and clearly.*

As the King of Hearts explains to the White Rabbit in *Alice in Wonderland*:

> Begin at the beginning, and go on till you
> come to the end; then stop.

The Greek word for "far away" is *tele*. What invention lets you

1) have a closer look at the moon

2) watch a baseball game in another city

3) talk to a friend in another country

4) use a distant computer

5) photograph a woodpecker on a faraway tree

6) beam yourself up to the spaceship (at least in movies!)

ANSWERS

WORDS FROM *TELE*

1) telescope (Greek *skopein*, to look at)

2) television (Latin *videre*, to see)

3) telephone (Greek *phonein*, to speak)

4) teleprocessing, or telecommunications (Latin *processus*, process, or to communicate)

5) telephoto lens (Greek *phos*, light)

6) teleportation (Latin *portare*, to carry)

18 LOOKING FORWARD

Close to four hundred million people speak English as their native language. As many again learned it as a second language. Another seven or eight hundred million have studied the language. All in all, perhaps a quarter of the people on earth have some ability to speak and understand English.

And many more would like to. After all, English opens the door to travel, to the Internet, to everything from leading-edge science to the latest Hollywood blockbusters.

What will happen to it in the years to come?

Will English continue to grow and spread, displacing all other languages, as people around the globe become more tightly linked by instant communications? Will other languages wither away as nations become more dependent on this common speech of technology and trade?

Or will English fragment into many different languages, the way Latin split into Italian and Spanish and French? Is this happening already?

Consider the Caribbean island of Jamaica, colonized first by Spain and later by England. Around 1640, the first shiploads of Africans were taken there to work as slaves in the sugar plantations. Over the centuries, a Jamaican form of English has developed. The words are mostly English but they are said differently, and linked by African-style grammar. Some words are specifically Jamaican – *winjy* for "sickly," *duppy* for "ghost," *braata* for "a little extra," *bangarang* for "a big fuss," *peeny wally* for "firefly." The result is almost incomprehensible to outsiders. In colonial days, this local speech was dismissed as ignorant and inferior. But today Jamaica is an independent country, and many people say this is their true national language. Will other new languages grow out of English in the same way? Will they eventually replace it?

Perhaps the upset will be more dramatic. Perhaps English will be swept aside by the preferred language of some new superpower. Will it be Chinese, already spoken by a billion or so people? Or Spanish, the language of hundreds of millions in Europe and the Americas? Or will it be some other language that we can't yet imagine being a competitor? Will the world's anglophones scramble to master this vital new language, and end up speaking English only to their children and their dogs?

The growth of English has depended on so many twists of fate: Rome's invincible armies, the rise of Christianity, the Vikings in their dragon boats, the shocking victory of William and his Norman cavalry, the Black Death, the religious conflict that drove the Pilgrims to North America. Who knows what events will shape it in the future? Or what triumphs or catastrophes will drive other languages?

But for the past thousand years and more, through conquest and through defeat, English has grown amazingly strong and subtle and versatile. The power of the language, and our ability to use it, affects our whole lives. Language – any language – is not just a tool for getting through the day, for chatting and arguing and reading the TV listings. It's the foundation of society, the bond between us that lets us work together and cooperate and share. "Speech is civilization itself," said a German novelist. "The word, even the most contradictory word, preserves contact."

The way we speak shapes the very way we think. "Language is the dress of thought," said Samuel Johnson. "Words are absolutely necessary for thinking," noted another writer, "and with a minimum of words there is a minimum of thought."

Our speech also determines our ability to change the thinking of others. Whatever we have in our hearts and minds, we need language to express it. "Axes and atom bombs can change the material world," declared a British scientist, "but only language can alter human ideas."

But let's leave the last word to *My Fair Lady*'s cranky Professor Higgins, as he urges Eliza the flowerseller to speak English well, to honor its beauty and power and its wealth of history:

Remember that you are a human being with a soul and the divine gift of articulate speech; that your native language is the language of Shakespeare and Milton and the Bible; and don't sit there crooning like a bilious pigeon.

TIMELINE
(most dates are approximate)

BCE

2500s early Britons build Stonehenge

700s Celts begin migrating from Europe to England

55 Julius Caesar leads first of two expeditions to Britain

CE

43 Romans invade Britain, bringing Latin language

400s Romans withdraw from Britain; Angles, Saxons, and others invade, bringing Germanic languages

600s Anglo-Saxons are spread across much of Britain

800 Vikings (Norse, Danes) begin raiding Britain and France

865 Vikings begin settling in England

871 Alfred the Great becomes king, unites Anglo-Saxon England

911 Vikings in France win their own dukedom, Normandy

1000 earliest surviving copy of *Beowulf* is written

1066 Normans conquer England, bringing Norman French

1340 birth of Chaucer (d. 1400)

1348 Black Death sweeps Britain (and returns later)

1384 Wycliffe's hand-written English-language Bible is published

1400s English is again the official language of England

1476 Caxton sets up England's first printing press

1525 Tyndale publishes New Testament in English

1564 birth of Shakespeare (d. 1616)

1600s England begins gaining power in India

1607 Jamestown, first permanent English settlement in America, is founded

1755 Johnson publishes his dictionary in England

1776 thirteen American colonies rebel against England

1787 first convict ships sail to Australia

1800s British Empire extends around the world

1828 Webster publishes his dictionary in America

मः पुरटकं पठनु

"Let him read a book."

MORE ABOUT SANSKRIT

Sanskrit is the classical language of ancient India. An early version was spoken some thirty-five hundred years ago; long before Indo-Europeans learned to write, Hindu religious texts called the Veda were recited and sung from memory. By 400 BCE, classical Sanskrit was the language of Hindu culture and romantic literature, including lengthy poems about love and adventure, and fables and fairy tales. (**Sanskrit** comes from *samskrta*, "perfected." *Veda* is Sanskrit for "knowledge," from the same root as Old English *witan*, "know.")

Sanskrit uses a much larger alphabet than English, and a lot of special marks to show how words are pronounced. The language is complex and highly inflected (words change depending on how they're used). It has eight cases for nouns, three genders (masculine, feminine, and neuter), and three numbers (not only singular and plural but also dual, for talking about just two things or two people).

Today a simpler language, Hindi – which comes from Sanskrit – is India's official language. Sanskrit is used mostly in the temples. It's often written in a Hindi alphabet called Devanagari, in which the letters of a word are spelled from left to right, as in English, but joined together. Sanskrit numbers look similar to ours: १ २ ३ – but the words for **one two three**, pronounced *eka, dvi, tri*, are written: एक दि त्रि.

"The art of speaking enchants the soul."

Ψυχαγωγιαν ουσαν

MORE ABOUT GREEK

Like Sanskrit, Greek (or something close to it) was spoken at least thirty-five hundred years ago. Greek writing probably developed about five hundred years later. Again like Sanskrit, classical Greek is highly inflected, with words changing according to how they're used. But the Greek uses a much simpler alphabet of about twenty-four letters (a few letters came and went over the years). In fact, the Greek alphabet is much like ours, although some of the letters look a little different.

our spelling		Greek spelling
one	*en*	ἑν
two	*duo*	δυο
three	*treis*	τρεις

Here are some Greek words from chapter 4, in English spelling. Can you match up the English spelling with the Greek? (Hint: the letter *e* has two forms, depending on how it's said.)

delta	(the letter d)	δημος
demos	(people)	μεγας
kuklos	(circle)	δελτα
megas	(big)	κυκλος

Greek does have some tricky bits – *ph* and *th* are combined into single letters, the letter *h* is shown by punctuation (ʽεν, above, is pronounced "hen,") the *r* looks like our *p*, the *p* looks like a little table, and so on – but it doesn't take long to learn the alphabet. Here are some harder words from chapter 3 – can you match them up?

helios	(sun)	θεος
krokodilos	(crocodile)	πυρ
pur	(fire)	ʽηλιος
theos	(god)	κροκοδιλος

The ancient Greeks also had capital letters, though they're a bit harder to recognize. As well, they used their letters in their numbering system. Here's the whole alphabet.

	capitals	small letters	
alpha	A	α	*a* as in *bat* or *saw*
beta	B	β	*b*
gamma	Γ	γ	*g* as in *go*
delta	Δ	δ	*d*
epsilon	E	ε	*e* as in *get*
zeta	Z	ζ	*z*
eta	H	η	*e* like *a* in *paper*

theta	Θ	ϑ	*th*
iota	I	ι	*i*
kappa	K	κ	*k*
lambda	Λ	λ	*l*
mu	M	μ	*m*
nu	N	ν	*n*
xi	Ξ	ξ	*x*
omikron	O	ο	*o* as in *pot*
pi	Π	π	*p*
rho	P	ρ	*r*
sigma	Σ	σ or ς	*s*
tau	T	τ	*t*
upsilon	Υ	υ	*u* as in *pull*
phi	Φ	φ	*ph*
khi	X	χ	*kh*
psi	Ψ	ψ	*ps*
omega	Ω	ω	*o* as in *roll*

Modern Greek looks very similar to the Greek of classical times, but the pronunciation has changed, as it has in English.

In the old days, Greek could be written left to right, right to left, or weaving back and forth in a style called "boustrophedon" – meaning the way an ox (*bous*, or βους) plows a field, from one side to the other and then back again:

> an ox plows a field from
> rehto eht ot edis eno
> and then back again

VIRTUS MILITUM FUIT ADMODUM LAUDANDA

"The excellence of our soldiers was most laudable."

MORE ABOUT LATIN

About twenty-five hundred years ago, Latini people lived around Roma, in Italy. As these Romans conquered their neighbors, their language, Latin, spread through Italy and beyond. But there were two versions of Latin – the classical kind, for writing and fine speeches, and a simpler "vulgar" kind (from Latin *vulgus*, "common people"), which most people spoke. Sometimes the two were quite different. For example, **cat** was *feles* in classical Latin but *cattus* in common Latin; borrowing from both versions, we can talk about either "cats" or "felines." Over time, common Latin disintegrated into Romance languages like French and Spanish. Classical Latin was preserved in the works of great writers across Europe, although it hasn't been anyone's mother tongue for over a thousand years.

The Romans used an alphabet of twenty-three capital letters (Latin was always written in capitals at that time):

A B C D E F G H I K L M N O P Q R S T V X Y Z

They had no *J*, which is a variety of *I* – our word "eject" comes from *iactare*, "to throw." They had no *W*, and *U* and *V* were the same letter (notice that our letter shaped like two *V*s is called "double-*U*," not "double-*V*").

Roman Latin was highly inflected, but it didn't have as many versions of nouns as Greek or Sanskrit. There were no dual forms, for one thing – just singular and plural. But some verbs changed dramatically depending on how they were used, and studying Latin means memorizing four "principal parts" for every verb. For the Latin word meaning "give," those parts are *do, dare, dedi, datus*:

<u>I</u> give	*do* (the root of English **donate**)
<u>to</u> give	*dare*
<u>I have</u> given	*dedi*
<u>having been</u> given	*datus* (the root of English **date**)

So English "donate" and "date" come from Latin *dare*, and look different because the verb is inflected – yet our verb "to dare" doesn't come from *dare* at all, but from an Old English word, *durran*.

Ðy mara wisdom wære ðy we ma geðeoda cunnon.

"There will be more wisdom, the more languages we know."

MORE ABOUT OLD ENGLISH

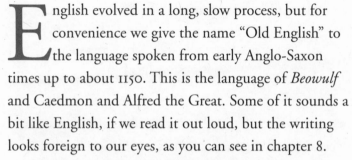

English evolved in a long, slow process, but for convenience we give the name "Old English" to the language spoken from early Anglo-Saxon times up to about 1150. This is the language of *Beowulf* and Caedmon and Alfred the Great. Some of it sounds a bit like English, if we read it out loud, but the writing looks foreign to our eyes, as you can see in chapter 8.

By 1150, English had expanded and borrowed a lot from Norman French. The language from 1150 until about 1500 is called Middle English, and this is what Chaucer used – more like the language we know, but still not easy to read.

When printed books appeared around 1500, they helped pull the language together into Modern English – the language of Shakespeare's plays and the King James Bible, which are readable and familiar even though they were written hundreds of years ago.

The earliest Anglo-Saxon writings we have are in futhark, an alphabet of signs called "runes." The runes are made almost entirely of straight lines, and futhark was probably used mostly for carving short inscriptions –

perhaps a few words on a coin or a stone, or the blade of a sword. (The name comes from the first six letters – *th* is a single letter – just as our alphabet is named for alpha, beta.)

Almost all manuscripts written in Old English use a later alphabet. It's much like the Roman alphabet, with a few letters missing and a few extras added. *A* and *E* could be written together (*Æ*) in a sign called a ligature, to mean a sound like the *a* in "cat." Ð (eth) and þ (thorn) stood for the *th* sound in "cloth" or "clothes." ƿ (wynn) is confusingly similar to thorn, but it represents a *w* sound. The alphabet looked something like this:

Aa Ææ Bb Ⅼc Dꝺ Ðð Ꞓe Fꝼ Ᵹᵹ Ⱨh Ⅰı Ll
ꟿm Nn Oo Pp Rꞃ Ꞅꞃꞅ Tꞇ Uu ƿƿ Xx Vẏ Ᵽþ

As time went by, spellings gradually changed: *ac* and *bat* became **oak** and **boat**, *scip* became **ship**, *ecg* became **edge**. The letters *h* and *w* might change places (*hwael* became **whale**, *hwil* became **while**); an *h* before a consonant might be dropped (*hrof* became **roof**, *hlot* became **lot**); and so on.

While the verbs could still be complicated, Old English was less inflected than Sanskrit or Greek or Latin. Nouns had only four cases, though they still came in singular and plural, and masculine, feminine, and neuter. As time went by, English-speakers were more and more likely to use prepositions to show exactly what they meant – "<u>to</u> my friend, <u>from</u> my friend" – instead of changing the word endings.

In grammar as well as vocabulary, English was growing close to the language we know today.

SOURCE NOTES

Publisher and date are given where a book is first referred to, unless the book is a classic or is included in the Selected Bibliography. All Shakespeare quotations are from two volumes of *The Complete Pelican Shakespeare: The Comedies and the Romances* and *The Tragedies* (London: Penguin, 1969). I have relied extensively on the *Oxford Dictionary of English Etymology*, the *Canadian Oxford Dictionary*, and *The Oxford Companion to English Literature*.

The early history of Britain and the English language is still in dispute, and sources often differ. I have tried to speak generally where details are contested.

The epigraph is from *Thorndale*.

Introduction: The Puzzle of English
Bilbo's speech is from Chapter 1 of *The Hobbit, or There and Back Again*, by J.R.R. Tolkien (London: Unwin, 1970). Bryson notes in *The Mother Tongue* that the number of English words depends on whether **mouse** and **mice** are two words, whether computer **mouse** and field **mouse** are one word, and so on. The homophonic spelling quizzes are based on *The Story of English*, by McCrum, Cran, and MacNeil, and *Alpha Beta*, by John Man.

Chapter 1 The Mother Tongue

The table of numbers is drawn partly from *Inventing English*, by Lerer.

Chapter 2 The Glory That Was Greece

Thanks to Roberta Shaw at the Royal Ontario Museum for correcting the caption about the priest Khenu's tomb at Sakkara, Egypt. The Plato quotes are from *Phaedrus*, sec. 271, and *Apologia of Socrates*, sec. 18, respectively.

Chapter 5 Amicus, Amice, Amicum

The magic spells are from chapter 12 of *Harry Potter and the Prisoner of Azkaban*, by J.K. Rowling (Vancouver: Raincoast, 1999).

Chapter 6 Angles and Saxons and Vikings

The quotes "ivories and jewelled crucifixes" and "'From the fury'" are from *Set in a Silver Sea*, by Bryant.

Chapter 7 Alfred and the Vikings

"There will be more wisdom" is from the prose preface of King Alfred's translation of Pope Gregory the Great's *Pastoral Care*. The comparison of English and Norse words is from *The Year 1000*, by Lacey and Danziger.

Chapter 8 Riddles, Hymns, and Tales of Battle

The riddle-verses are numbers 23 and 65 in *The Exeter Book Riddles*, translated by Crossley-Holland. The *Beowulf* translation has been tweaked to emphasize resemblances to English words, for the sake of comprehension. (The meaning of *fagne* is closer to "decorated" – in this context, probably with blood!) The quote for the year 871 in *The Anglo-Saxon Chronicles* is based on a translation by Professor Harvey De Roo.

Chapter 9 The Defeat of the English

The thesaurus referred to is *Thesaurus of English Words and Phrases* (revised), by Peter Mark Roget (London: Longman's, 1959).

Chapter 10 Tales of Cnihts and Fair Ladies

The story of kohl is drawn from *The Meaning of Tingo*, by Jacot de Boinod. The quote "high and low" is from Professor Nevill Coghill, cited in *English Life in Chaucer's Day*, by Hart. The quote "cursed and complained" is from *The Meaning of Everything*, by Winchester.

Chapter 11 How to Spell It? How to Say It?

The remarks on Caxton, and the Caxton quote, are drawn from *The Story of English*, by McCrum, Cran, and MacNeil. *The Mother Tongue*, by Bryson, attributes Caxton's story to Caxton's preface to

Eneydos (1490), and is also the source of the comment on *Grammatica Linguae Anglicanae*.

Chapter 12 Making the "Good Book" Better
The Ruth quote is from Ruth, 1:16.

Chapter 13 Gloriana and the Bard
The bishop advocating "gothroughsome" was Reginald Pecock. Some details about Shakespeare are drawn from *Shakespeare*, by Bryson. Petruchio's words are from Act II Scene i. Lear's words are from Act II Scene iv. Richard's words are from Act V Scene iii. References to *Macbeth*'s "weird" witches are in Act II Scene i, Act III Scene i, and Act IV Scene i. The number of different words used by Shakespeare is disputed.

Chapter 14 Greener Pastures
Native American words could be similar across several languages, so it's often not clear which version was adapted into English. Much of the Newfoundland section is from *The Dictionary of Newfoundland English*, edited by G.M. Story and others (Toronto: University of Toronto Press, 1982). The Mather quote is from *Decennium Luctuosum*, cited in *Narratives of the Indian Wars*, 1675-1699, edited by Charles H. Lincoln (New York: Barnes & Noble, 1913). All Franklin quotes are from *Benjamin Franklin: A Biography in His Own Words*, edited by Joseph L. Gardner, in the Founding Fathers series (New York: Newsweek/ Harper & Row, 1972). Some of the Tok Pisin is drawn from *Pidgin Phrasebook: Pidgin Languages of Oceania*, by Trevor Balzer and others (Hawthorn, Australia: Lonely Planet, 1999). Tok Pisin is now gaining a place as a first language, becoming a creole rather than a pidgin language.

Chapter 15 The War between English and English
The Webster quotes, "There iz no alternativ," from an essay, and "A *national* language," from a 1786 letter, are cited in *The Long Journey of Noah Webster*, by Rollins. The Swift quote is from *A Proposal for Correcting, Improving and Ascertaining the English Tongue...*, addressed to the Earl of Oxford and Mortimer (London: Benj. Tooke, 1712). The Johnson quote, "barbarous corruptions, . . ." is cited in *Blooming English*, by Burridge. Some remarks on the *Oxford English Dictionary*, including the quote "fat, heavy," are from *The Meaning of Everything*, by Winchester. The Humpty Dumpty quote is from chapter 6 of *Alice through the Looking-Glass*, by Lewis Carroll.

Chapter 16 Britannia's Heyday

"Our tongue is known" is from "Old England Is Our Home," by Mary Howitt. The Humpty Dumpty quote is from chapter 6 of *Alice through the Looking-Glass*. The example of rhyming slang is from "The New Pig's Ears," by Soraya Roberts, in the *National Post*, January 4, 2007.

Chapter 17 Words, Words, Words

The statistics on new words per year are extrapolated from *The New York Times*, April 3, 1989, cited in *The Mother Tongue*, by Bryson. The origin of "googol" and "googolplex" is from Wikipedia; Milton Sirotta was the nephew of Edward Kasner. The King of Hearts quote is from chapter 12 of *Alice's Adventures in Wonderland*, by Lewis Carroll.

Chapter 18 Looking Forward

Remarks on the dominance of English are based partly on *Empires of the Word*, by Ostler. Much of the Jamaican material is drawn from *The Story of English*, by McCrum, Cran, and MacNeil. The Johnson quote is from his *Lives of the Poets: Cowper*. The quote from German novelist Thomas Mann is cited in *The Miracle of Language*, by Lederer, as are those from "another writer," Aubrey A. Douglas, and British scientist H.C. Lonquet-Higgins. Professor Higgins's speech is from Act I of *Pygmalion*, by George Bernard Shaw, and is also in the film *My Fair Lady*.

More about Sanskrit, Greek, Latin, Old English

All these languages evolved over many centuries, across their various regions. The Julius Caesar quote is from *Commentaries of Caesar on the Gallic War*, Book V (New York: David McKay, 1963), author's translation.

SELECTED BIBLIOGRAPHY
* suggested reading

Abrams, M.H. (editor), and others. *The Norton Anthology of English Literature*, Volume 1, fourth edition. New York: Norton, 1962.

Barber, Katherine, editor. *Canadian Oxford Dictionary*, second edition. Don Mills, Ontario: Oxford University Press, 2004.

*Branigan, Keith. *Roman Britain: Life in an Imperial Province*. London: Reader's Digest Association, 1980.

Bryant, Arthur. A History of Britain and the British People, Volume 1: *Set in a Silver Sea*. London: Grafton, 1985.

——. A History of Britain and the British People, Volume 2: *Freedom's Own Island*. London: Grafton, 1987.

Bryson, Bill. *The Mother Tongue: English and How It Got That Way*. New York: William Morrow, 1990.

——. *Shakespeare: The World As Stage*. (Eminent Lives.) New York: HarperCollins, 2007.

Burridge, Kate. *Blooming English*. Cambridge: Cambridge University Press, 2004.

Chickering, Howell D., Jr., translator. *Beowulf: A Dual-Language Edition*. New York: Doubleday, 1977.

Crossley-Holland, Kevin, translator. *The Exeter Book Riddles* (revised). London: Penguin, 1993.

Drabble, Margaret. *The Oxford Companion to English Literature*, fifth edition. Oxford: Oxford University Press, 1985.

Fatsis, Stefan. *Word Freak: Heartbreak, Triumph, Genius, amd Obsession in the World of Competitive Scrabble Players*. New York: Penguin, 2002.

Gaur, Albertine. *A History of Writing*. New York: Cross River Press, 1992.

*Hart, Roger. *English Life in Chaucer's Day*. London: Wayland, 1973.

Hitchings, Henry. *The Secret Life of Words: How English Became English*. New York: Farrar, Straus and Giroux, 2008.

*Humez, Alexander and Nicholas. *Alpha and Omega: The Life and Times of the Greek Alphabet*. London: Kudos and Godine, 1983.

*———. *Latin for People: Latina pro Populo*. Boston: Little, Brown, 1976.

*Jacot de Boinod, Adam. *The Meaning of Tingo and Other Extraordinary Words from around the World*. New York: Penguin Press, 2006.

Kurlansky, Mark. *Salt: A World History*. Toronto: Knopf, 2002.

*Lacey, Robert, and Danny Danziger. *The Year 1000: What Life Was Like at the Turn of the First Millennium*. New York: Little, Brown, 1999.

Lass, Abraham H., David Kiremidjian, Ruth M. Goldstein. *Dictionary of Allusions*. London: Sphere, 1989.

*Lederer, Richard. *The Miracle of Language*. New York: Pocket Books, 1991.

Lerer, Seth. *Inventing English: A Portable History of the Language*. New York: Columbia University Press, 2007.

*McCrum, Robert, William Cran, Robert MacNeil. *The Story of English* (revised edition). London: Faber and Faber, 1992.

*Man, John. *Alpha Beta: How Our Alphabet Changed the Western World*. London: Headline, 2000.

*Manguel, Alberto. *A History of Reading*. Toronto: Knopf, 1996.

Michaelson, O.V. *Words at Play: Quips, Quirks & Oddities*. New York: Sterling, 1997.

Mitchell, Bruce, and Fred C. Robinson. *A Guide to Old English*. Toronto: University of Toronto Press, 1982.

Onions, C.T., editor. *Oxford Dictionary of English Etymology*. Oxford: Oxford University Press, 1996.

Ostler, Nicholas. *Empires of the Word: A Language History of the World*. New York: HarperCollins, 2005.

Rollins, Richard M. *The Long Journey of Noah Webster*. Philadelphia: University of Pennsylvania Press, 1980.

*Ross, Val. *You Can't Read This: Forbidden Books, Lost Writing, Mistranslations and Codes*. Toronto: Tundra, 2006.

*Savage, Anne (translator). *The Anglo-Saxon Chronicles: The Authentic Voices of England, from the Time of Julius Caesar to the Coronation of Henry II*. Godalming, UK: CLB, 1997.

*Winchester, Simon. *The Meaning of Everything: The Story of the Oxford English Dictionary*. Oxford: Oxford University Press, 2003.

PICTURE SOURCES

MVM: original art by Margrieta Vandelis-Muir
TRL: courtesy of the Toronto Reference Library

Page 9, MVM; 10, photo courtesy of W. Peter Gorrell; 11, MVM; 12, TRL; 15, 18, 19, MVM; 20, TRL; 21, 26, 30, 31, MVM; 33, TRL; 34, MVM; 37, 41, 43, TRL; 46, MVM; 47, TRL; 48, MVM; 52, 55, 56, 59, 60, TRL; 67, MVM; 70, TRL; 71, by kind permission of David Betts; 75, 77, 80, TRL; 82 top, MVM; 82 bottom, Library of Congress, LC-USZ62-15195; 94 left, MVM; 103, by kind permission of the artist, Thomas E. Brown; 104, 105, photos courtesy of W. Peter Gorrell; 112, 121, MVM.

ACKNOWLEDGMENTS

My thanks to Kathy Lowinger, publisher of Tundra
Books, and Carolyn Jackson, my editor, for their patience
and fortitude; to Professor Harvey De Roo for all his help
and enlightenment regarding the Old English material;
and to John Elmslie of the Toronto Reference Library and
Susan Meisner for their special expertise. I am indebted to
Margrieta Vandelis-Muir for the time and care she put
into the maps and other original artwork. Professor Andy
Orchard, of the Centre for Medieval Studies at the University of Toronto, very generously read the manuscript
and pointed out my lapses into ignorance; any remaining
errors are, of course, entirely my own fault.

– G.K.G.

INDEX

Christianity, 22, 30, 32-33, 35, 37, 38, 45, 52, 66-73, 119; Anglican Church (Church of England), 32, 69, 71, 74, 75; Catholic Church, 32, 36, 50, 66-68, 70, 74, 75; Protestant movement,68-69, 70

Columbus, Christopher, 70

Crusades, 52

Danes, *see* Vikings

Danish, 6

Dark Ages, 32

Dictionaries, 93-96, 101; Noah Webster's, 95; *Oxford English Dictionary*, 95; Samuel Johnson's, 93-95

Dutch, 5, 6, 7, 83; influence of on English, 83

East India Company, 104-105

Edward the Confessor, King (England), 45-46

Egbert, King of Wessex, 33

Egypt, 8, 10

Egyptian, ancient, 9; hieroglyphs, 9, 11

Elizabeth I, Queen (England), 71, 74-76, 77, 81, 104

Elizabeth II, Queen (United Kingdom), 51

England, 8, 18, 33, 36, 45-48, 52, 66-71, 74-76, 81; Black Death in, 57, 68, 76; civil war in, 52; during reign of Elizabeth I, 74-76, 81; Industrial Revolution in, 103; London, 22, 30, 35, 36, 48; Normans in, 45-51, 52, 54, 57, 112

English language: adjectives in, 25; apostrophe in, 26; becomes the accepted language in England, 44, 56-57; and changes to alpha-bet, 54; confusion of words in, 99-100; future of, 118-21; gender in, 25; and the "great vowel shift," 62-63; influence of tourism on, 102, 103-107,110; influence of war on, 112-14; invented words in, 107-108; nouns in, 25-26; plurals in, 25, 26; posses sive case in, 26; prepositions in, 26; rate of new words entering the language, 116; and scientific language, 115; standardization of, 60, 61, 93-95; word order in, 26; *see also* Middle English; Old English

English language, influence of other languages on, 1-3, 6, 51; ancient Greek, 13-14, 16; Arabic, 53-54; Celtic, 19, 22; Dutch, 83; French, 48-49; German, 106-107; Hindi, 105; Latin, 20, 21-22, 27, 50; native languages, 3, 83, 88; Old Norse, 38-39; Scandinavian languages, 54; Yiddish, 115

English literature, 41-44, 54-56, 76-80; *Beowulf*, 42-43, 52, 131; *Caedmon's Hymn*, 42, 55; *Canterbury Tales*, 55, 60; "I Have a Young Sister," 56; Shakespeare's plays, 76-80

Ethelbert, King of Kent, 32

Etheldrida, see Audrey, Saint

France, 19, 23, 30, 52, 57, 74, 75, 81, 82, 83, 110; French Revolution, 102; Viking raids on, 33-35, 45

Franklin, Benjamin, 87-88; *Poor Richard's Almanack*, 88

French, 5, 6, 7, 23, 50, 54, 56, 57, 58, 65, 69, 72, 86, 91, 95, 119, 129; Norman version of, 45, 48, 50, 51; slang, 110